NEW VANGUARD • 164

GERMAN BATTLESHIPS 1914–18 (1)

Deutschland, Nassau and *Helgoland* classes

GARY STAFF   ILLUSTRATED BY PAUL WRIGHT

First published in Great Britain in 2009 by Osprey Publishing,
Midland House, West Way, Botley, Oxford, OX2 0PH, UK
44-02 23rd St, Suite 219, Long Island City, NY 11101, USA
E-mail: info@ospreypublishing.com

A CIP catalogue record for this book is available from the British Library.

ISBN: 978 1 84603 467 1
E-book ISBN: 978 1 84908 258 7

Page layout by: Melissa Orrom Swan, Oxford
Index by Alan Thatcher
Typeset in Sabon and Myriad Pro
Originated by PPS Grasmere, Leeds, UK
Printed in China through Worldprint Ltd

10 11 12 13 14   10 9 8 7 6 5 4 3 2 1

FOR A CATALOGUE OF ALL BOOKS PUBLISHED BY OSPREY MILITARY
AND AVIATION PLEASE CONTACT:

NORTH AMERICA
Osprey Direct, c/o Random House Distribution Center, 400 Hahn
Road, Westminster, MD 21157
E-mail: uscustomerservice@ospreypublishing.com

ALL OTHER REGIONS
Osprey Direct, The Book Service Ltd, Distribution Centre, Colchester
Road, Frating Green, Colchester, Essex, CO7 7DW
E-mail: customerservice@ospreypublishing.com

Osprey Publishing is supporting the Woodland Trust, the UK's leading
woodland conservation charity, by funding the dedication of trees.

www.ospreypublishing.com

CONTENTS

GERMAN BATTLESHIPS 1914–18 (1)
DEUTSCHLAND, NASSAU AND HELGOLAND CLASSES

INTRODUCTION

Prior to 1871, Germany did not exist as an independent country. In its place were numerous states, the largest of which were Prussia, Bavaria and Würtemburg. After the successful campaign against France in 1871, these states were united into the German Empire and the first Emperor, or Kaiser, of the unified Second Reich was Kaiser Wilhelm I. Previously the German states had neither the will nor means to support a modern navy, and Kaiser Wilhelm I also lacked enthusiasm for this branch of the military services. It was only after the enthronement of his son Wilhelm II in 1888 that this attitude changed, and from 1890 to 1901 no fewer than 19 battleships were laid down. In 1897, Wilhelm named Admiral Alfred von Tirpitz the State Secretary of the Reichsmarineamt (Naval Office; RMA), and within a year he inaugurated a long-term fleet-building programme. The first Fleet Law was passed in 1898 and made the Kaiser's desire for a new modern navy a legally binding state policy. It called for a fleet of 19 battleships, to be replaced after a lifespan of 25 years. The second Fleet Law of 1900 saw a doubling of the battleship numbers, and in future the German Fleet would consist of 38 battleships, 14 large cruisers and 38 small cruisers. This expansion seemed a natural step in view of Germany's expanding overseas empire.

Around the turn of the century, the Design Department of the RMA designed the battleships of the *Braunschweig* class. In contrast to their predecessors, they returned to a 28cm calibre main armament, after the firm Krupp succeeded in developing quick-loading technology for this calibre. With this class the Germans had reached the limits of both development and displacement. Any further expansions in size would necessitate enormous cost increases for infrastructure, such as enlarging slipways and docks, deepening channels around the harbours and deepening and widening the Kaiser Wilhelm Canal and its locks. According to the Fleet Law of 1900, the budget of 1904 would allow for five ships – constituting the later *Deutschland* class – and they were to be practically repeats of the *Braunschweig* class. The two classes together were the last pre-dreadnought battleships of the Imperial Navy.

BATTLESHIPS OF THE *DEUTSCHLAND* CLASS

The *Linienschiffe* (lit. 'ships of the line'), or battleships of the *Braunschweig* class, were designed in 1900–01, and were followed closely in 1901–02 by the design for the *Deutschland* class. The first ship of the class, *Deutschland*, was almost identical in every way to its predecessors. The armour thickness and distribution were the same, with the belt armour being 225mm thick and the casemates 160mm. The boiler plant was also the same, with eight naval Schulz-Thornycroft boilers and six cylindrical boilers. The one small difference was that the four 17cm medium-calibre guns mounted in turrets on the upper deck of the *Braunschweig* class were replaced by casemates on the upper deck in the *Deutschland* class.

After the *Deutschland*, however, the remaining ships of the *Deutschland* class were built to a modified design. The six cylindrical boilers were replaced by four naval boilers of the Schulz-Thornycroft design, now giving a total of 12 naval boilers. The thickness of the armoured plate was also increased: the belt armour was increased from 225mm to 240mm, and the citadel armour was increased from 160mm to 170mm.

The last two classes of German pre-dreadnought battleships represented excellent value for money and were equal to their foreign contemporaries. They were used in the front line during the war, and provided excellent service.

	Deutschland	Hannover	Pommern	Schlesien	Schleswig-Holstein
Building dockyard	Germania, Kiel	Imperial, Wilhelmshaven	A.G. Vulcan, Stettin	F. Schichau, Danzig	Germania, Kiel
Building number	109	28	262	751	113
Keel laying	20 July 1903	7 November 1904	22 March 1904	19 November 1904	18 August 1905
Launched	19 November 1904	29 May 1905	2 December 1905	28 May 1906	17 December 1906
Commissioned	3 August 1906	1 October 1907	6 August 1907	5 May 1908	6 July 1908
Displacement (tonnes)	Designed: 13,191 Loaded: 14,218	Designed: 13,191 Loaded: 14,218	Designed: 13,191 Loaded: 14,218	Designed: 13,191 Loaded: 14,218	Designed: 13,191 Loaded: 14,218
Length (metres)	127.6	127.6	127.6	127.6	127.6
Beam (metres)	22.2	22.2	22.2	22.2	22.2
Draught (metres)	Construction: 8.21 Loaded: 8.25	Construction: 8.21 Loaded: 8.25	Construction: 8.21 Loaded: 8.25	Construction: 8.21 Loaded: 8.25	Construction: 8.21 Loaded: 8.25
Performance (indicated horsepower)	Designed: 16,000 Maximum: 16,990	Designed: 16,000 Maximum: 17,768	Designed: 16,000 Maximum: 17,696	Designed: 16,000 Maximum: 18,923	Designed: 16,000 Maximum: 19,330
Revolutions per minute	111	114	118	119	122
Speed (knots)	18.6	18.5	18.7	18.5	19.1
Fuel (tonnes) Supplemental oil firing from 1908–09	Construction: 700 Maximum: 1,540 Oil: 240	Construction: 700 Maximum: 1,540 Oil: 200	Construction: 850 Maximum: 1,740 Oil: 200	Construction: 850 Maximum: 1,740 Oil: 200	Construction: 850 Maximum: 1,740 Oil: 200
Range (nautical miles)	4,850nm at 10 knots	4,520nm at 10 knots	5,830nm at 10 knots	4,770nm at 10 knots	5,720nm at 10 knots
Cost (millions of gold marks)	24.5	24.2	24.6	24.9	24.9
Compartments	12	13	12	12	12
Double bottom (as percentage of length)	84	84	84	84	84
Crew	35 officers 708 men	35 officers 708 men	35 officers 708 men	35 officers 708 men	35 officers 708 men

Deutschland at speed during trials.

Armament

The armament of the *Deutschland* class consisted of 4 x 28cm SK (Schnelladenkanonen – 'quick-firing') L/40 cannon mounted in Drh.L C/01 turntable mounts. The cannon had a depression of -4° and elevation of +30°, giving them a maximum range of 188 hectometres (hm). Both the armour-piercing and high-explosive shells weighed 240kg and were fired with a muzzle velocity of 820 metres per second (mps). A total of 85 shells were carried for each barrel. The propellant charge came in a brass cartridge and weighed 73kg. A rate of fire of two projectiles per minute could be achieved.

Germany did not follow the lead of other nations and mount an intermediate-calibre gun in addition to the main- and medium-calibre guns. Instead they retained the medium-calibre armament, but on the *Braunschweig* and *Deutschland* classes the size of the medium-calibre battery was increased to 17cm. Nevertheless, the weight of *Deutschland's* broadside was around 1,600kg, whereas that of the British pre-dreadnought *King Edward VII* was around 2,400kg. *Deutschland* carried 14 x 17cm SK L/40 cannon in MPL C/01 pivot mounts. Munitions stowage amounted to 130 shells per gun; however, the guns were still worked manually, and, with the increase in calibre and consequent increase in weight of shell to around 75kg, high physical demands were placed on the serving crew. The understandable result was a rapid drop-off in the rate of fire, which was theoretically five shells per minute. Maximum range was 145hm.

The light artillery for defence against torpedo-boats and destroyers consisted of 20 x 8.8cm SK L/35 C/02 cannon in MPL C/02 mounts. Their 9kg shells could be fired at a rate of ten shots per minute and an outfit of 2,800 rounds was carried. In the summer of 1916, some of these guns were demounted and replaced with 4 x 8.8cm L/45 C/13 BAK (Ballonabwehrkanonen, lit. 'Balloon Defence Cannon') mounted on the aft superstructure. The range of these cannon was 141hm and rate of fire was 15 shots per minute.

The torpedo armament consisted of 6 x 45cm torpedo tubes, four mounted on the broadside, and one bow and one stern tube. The torpedoes were of the Bronze C/03 type with a warhead weight of 147.5kg and their range totalled 3,000m at 26 knots. A total outfit of 16 torpedoes was carried.

Armour

The first ship of this class, *Deutschland*, had a main belt armour 225mm thick, tapering to 140mm at its lower edge. The citadel armour had a thickness of 160mm. On the other ships of the class, the main belt was 240mm, tapering to 170mm at its lower edge, and the citadel armour was increased to 170mm. Deck armour was 40mm and the Böschung (sloping) armour was 67mm thick. Armour over the casemates was 35mm. The forward conning tower had a maximum thickness of 300mm and the aft conning tower had a maximum of 140mm. The 28cm turrets had frontal armour of 280mm, and a roof thickness of 50mm, while the barbettes had a maximum thickness of 250mm. The armour was Krupp cemented steel, a type of chrome-nickel steel.

Seakeeping

The ships of the *Deutschland* class were not such good sea boats as their predecessors, however, they were known to have decent seakeeping, with little pitching in a swell. They manoeuvred well and heeled 12° with hard-over rudder. With a metacentric height of 0.98m, they had a slow, gentle roll period.

Machinery

The *Deutschland* was outfitted with eight Schulz-Thornycroft boilers and six cylindrical boilers. The remainder of the class were fitted with 12 Schulz-Thornycroft boilers arranged in three boiler rooms. Supplemental oil firing was provided progressively. Steam was provided at 15 atmospheres, or 220psi, to three triple-expansion engines. The outboard shafts each drove a three-bladed 4.8m diameter propeller, and the centre engine drove a 4.5m diameter four-bladed propeller. The single rudder was operated by a steam engine.

To supply electrical current, there were four steam-driven turbo-generators manufactured by the company A.E.G. Each could provide 65kW of power at 110 volts, for a total output of 260kW. The *Deutschland* class also had an integral drainage system; two large-diameter pipes ran down each side of the lower ship and were serviced by several powerful drainage pump groups.

Hannover Frame 64

The armour of the *Hannover* was slightly thicker than the preceding *Brauschweig* class. The boilers were all of the Schulz-Thornycroft type.

General characteristics and changes

The ships of this class were difficult to distinguish from each other. Before the war, extra 110cm searchlights were added to the foremast and on pedestals adjacent to the foremost funnel. In 1914, observation positions were installed on both masts. Not all of the ships carried anti-torpedo nets.

Service record

Deutschland

Deutschland's keel was laid on 20 July 1903 at the Germania Dockyard in Kiel and was launched on 19 November 1904. The commissioning followed on 3 August 1906 and trials continued until the end of the following September. On 26 September, Admiral Prinz Heinrich, brother of the Kaiser, hoisted his flag in his new role as chief of the active battle fleet. He replaced Großadmiral von Koester and *Deutschland* began her role as fleet flagship. Tactically she was assigned to II Squadron.

In December 1906, the fleet undertook winter exercises in the North Sea and then returned to Kiel. With effect from 16 February 1907, the 'Active Battle Fleet' became known as the 'High Sea Fleet' at the suggestion of State Secretary Tirpitz, who wanted to avoid antagonizing the British, and so eliminated the aggressive term 'battle fleet' and abandoned any suggestion of a coastal defence fleet.

The battleship *Schlesien* resting between periods of duty guarding the Sound, the narrow stretch of water which provided the only entrance to the Baltic Sea..

7

A view of *Deutschland*'s funnels being painted by the crew. In the foreground are signal flags ready to hoist.

In early 1907 there was training in the North Sea, and in May–June tactical training in the same waters. A summer cruise to Norway followed, and then *Deutschland* went to Swinemünde, with autumn manoeuvres following in September. In November, *Deutschland* went to the dockyard for an annual overhaul.

The year 1908 began with exercises in the Baltic in February, and in May/June fleet exercises followed off Helgoland. As early as 1907, Prinz Heinrich had wanted to undertake training cruises in the Atlantic with the High Sea Fleet, to increase their battle readiness for long-distance overseas operations, and to give the crews an interesting interruption from the monotony of home waters. The idea came to nothing, however, initially because of political concerns, but then in 1908 the British fleet conducted a practice mobilization and in June carried out manoeuvres off the Danish coast. Prinz Heinrich now received approval for his plan, and on 13 July 1908 the High Sea Fleet passed through the Kaiser Wilhelm Canal into the North Sea, and then carried out tactical and strategic exercises in the Atlantic. During the manoeuvres, German ships visited various ports, and *Deutschland* visited Funchal and Santa Cruz de Tenerife. On 13 August, the fleet returned to Kiel. Autumn manoeuvres continued in September in the Baltic and North Sea, and a winter cruise took place in the Baltic.

The year 1909 went much as the previous year. An Atlantic cruise was conducted from 7 July to 1 August 1909, whereby *Deutschland* visited Bilbao. Autumn manoeuvres followed. At the end of 1909, during the annual overhaul period, the silhouette of *Deutschland* was altered by the addition of new searchlight pedestals and she also became the first ship of the navy to have an X-ray installation.

In May 1910 fleet exercises were conducted in the Kattegat, but the summer cruise went to Norwegian waters for the first time. Autumn manoeuvres followed. In November, the Kaiser enshipped aboard *Deutschland* for the opening of the Naval School at Flensburg-Mürwik. The year concluded with a fleet winter cruise in the western Baltic.

In 1911, the service was similar to the previous year – the summer manoeuvres were followed by a cruise to Norway and in autumn there were again manoeuvres in the Baltic. The winter of 1911, and the spring of 1912, went as usual but the 1912 summer cruise was only in Baltic waters, because of the Moroccan crisis. The autumn manoeuvres took place off Helgoland. On the return journey, *Deutschland* suffered a slight grounding in the Baltic, so that she had to be docked for repairs; she was able to take part in the winter cruise in November, however.

 SMS *DEUTSCHLAND*

The five ships of the *Deutschland* class were practically repeats of the previous *Braunschweig* class, apart from slightly heavier armour. The trend of foreign navies to adopt an intermediate calibre between the heavy- and medium-calibre cannon was not adopted, even though this meant the weight of the broadside was considerably less. The displacement of this class was limited by financial considerations, by the size of the harbours and docks, and especially by the limitations of the Kaiser Wilhelm Canal. With the leap in size and power to the first class of dreadnoughts, the *Deutschland* class lost its significance and was obsolete after only the type ship had been completed. Nevertheless, they represented good value for money, and were employed continuously throughout the war.

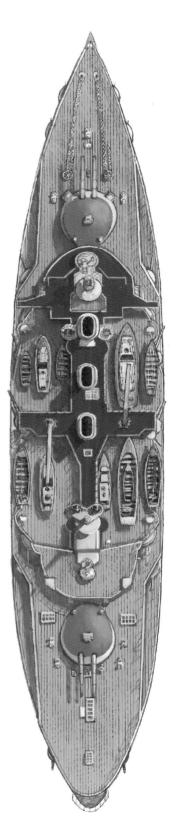

In January 1913, *Deutschland* was replaced as fleet flagship by *Friedrich der Große*. The golden bow decoration was removed and replaced by a heraldic shield. The ship now joined II Squadron and took part in all the manoeuvres up until the beginning of the war as part of this unit. With the outbreak of war in 1914, II Squadron went to guard the Elbe mouth, but from 2 to 23 October 1914 *Deutschland* lay in Kiel, and then went to the dockyard at Kiel from 27 October to 4 November. From 10 November to 12 November she undertook an advance to the east of Bornholm, and from 17 November she again lay off the Elbe mouth. *Deutschland* served in the picket and security service on Vosslapp Roads and on 15 February 1915 went to the lower Elbe for picket duty. A dockyard period followed in Kiel from 21 February to 12 March 1915, before returning to the Elbe.

Subsequent life for the *Deutschland* until spring 1916 was filled mainly with picket and security duty off the Elbe and Jade river mouths, interrupted by advances in support of light forces conducting mining operations. From 21 September to 11 October 1915, she went to the Baltic for training and then a dockyard period in Kiel. Further work followed in the Vulcan Dockyard in Hamburg from 27 February to 1 April 1916. On her return to Altenbruch Roads, *Deutschland* served as flagship for the chief of II Squadron, Konteradmiral Mauve. On 24–25 April 1916, II Squadron took part in the fleet advance to support the bombardment of Yarmouth and Lowestoft on the English coast, and on 4 May II Squadron supported the counterthrust against the British forces off Horns Reef.

Contrary to his previous intention, Vizeadmiral Scheer took the six ships of II Squadron into the Skagerrak battle. For *Deutschland* there were no engagements and after returning from the battle the squadron resumed picket and security duty on the Elbe mouth, and from time to time exchanged ships with the Sound watch in the Baltic. For *Deutschland*, this service continued until 27 July 1917 and was interrupted only by training periods and dockyard time. She lay in Kiel bay from 22 December 1916 to 16 January 1917, and from 24 January 1917 to 4 April 1917 was in the dockyard at Hamburg.

On 28 July 1917, *Deutschland* departed Altenbruch Roads and went to security duty in the western Baltic. On 15 August 1917, II Squadron was officially disbanded, and on 31 August *Deutschland* went to Kiel where on 10 September 1917 she was decommissioned.

After the ship was placed out of service, the guns were removed and *Deutschland* was transferred to Wilhelmshaven, where she served as an accommodation ship until the end of the war. She was stricken from the list of warships on 25 January 1920 and was wrecked in Wilhelmshaven.

Hannover

Namesake: Prussian province.

The second ship of the *Deutschland* class was approved for the 1904 budget and on 1 June 1904 the Imperial Dockyard, Wilhelmshaven, was granted the contract. The keel was laid on 7 November and launching followed on 29 September 1905.

On 1 October 1907, *Hannover* was commissioned and trials began, but these were interrupted in November by fleet exercises in the Skagerrak. Only on 13 February 1908 was *Hannover* detached from trials and assigned to II Squadron. In May–June, the spring exercises were undertaken in the North Sea and in July–August the Atlantic cruise of the fleet followed, where from 23 July to 1 August *Hannover* lay off Punta Delgado in the Azores. Autumn manoeuvres took place in September. After these, *Hannover* transferred from II Squadron to I Squadron, and served as squadron flagship there for two years. The year 1908 concluded with unit and fleet exercises in the Baltic in November.

Hannover took part in all the fleet exercises for 1909. In 1910 there were squadron exercises in February and on 1 April I Squadron moved from Kiel to Wilhelmshaven and subsequently took part in the spring manoeuvres, a summer cruise to Norway and the autumn manoeuvres.

In 1911 there were the typical fleet exercises in May, June and July–August. The Norwegian cruise followed and in August–September the autumn exercises. On 3 October, *Hannover*

Pommern in the Kaiser Wilhelm Canal. In the background is the Rendsburg Railway Viaduct.

transferred to II Squadron, and the year finished with exercises in November. In 1912 there were manoeuvres in February, March and April, but this year the summer cruise took place only in the Baltic. The autumn manoeuvres followed in August–September. For 1913 the summer cruise again went to Norway, and in November there were fleet exercises in the Baltic. For 1914 there were all the usual exercises and manoeuvres, and on 14 July 1914 the summer cruise again went to Norwegian waters. Because of the threat of war, however, the cruise was broken off prematurely. On 29 July 1914, II Squadron was back in Kiel and from there went to Wilhelmshaven.

During the days of mobilization in 1914, *Hannover* carried out security and readiness duties on Altenbruch Roads (Elbe mouth). In late October to early November, II Squadron vessels went to Kiel Dockyard to have modifications to their underwater protection system, in an attempt to make them more resistant to underwater damage. On 15–16 December, *Hannover* was part of the main body covering the cruiser raid on the English coast at Hartlepool, Scarborough and Whitby.

During the Dogger Bank battle on 24 January 1915, *Hannover* put to sea but nevertheless soon returned. On 17–18 April, *Hannover* belonged to a force covering II Aüfklarungsgruppe (AG; II Reconnaissance Group) when it laid a mine barrier off Swarte Bank, and she also took part in a result-less advance by Admiral von Pohl in the direction of Dogger Bank on 21–22 April. On 16 May, *Hannover* went to Kiel to change a 28cm gun barrel, but returned in time for the fleet advance 50 nautical miles north of Schiermonnikog Island – the advance was broken off prematurely because of poor weather. From 28 June to 12 July 1915, *Hannover* was again in Kiel Dockyard, this time to have supplemental oil firing fitted. On 11–12 September, *Hannover* and II Squadron covered a further minelaying operation by the II AG to Swarte Bank and on 23–24 October a further fleet advance was conducted without result.

With the fleet operation on 5–7 March 1916, *Hannover* and II Squadron remained back in the German Bight, ready in support. Yet they formed part of the main body for the operation of 24–25 April 1916 against Lowestoft and Great Yarmouth. The former commander of II Squadron, Vizeadmiral Scheer, took six ships of II Squadron to the Skagerrak battle. The squadron first opened fire in the evening and *Hannover* fired a total of eight 28cm shells and 22 x 17cm shells. She remained undamaged in the action.

After this battle, II Squadron resumed picket and security duty in the Elbe mouth. On 30 November 1916, however, the ships were discharged from the High Sea Fleet and the squadron was officially disbanded on 15 August 1917. *Hannover* went to Kiel for a period in dock on 4 November 1916 and then returned to the Elbe, but by early 1917 she was being used as a target ship in the Baltic. On 21 March 1917, some of her guns were dismounted and from 25 June to 16 September 1917 she was refitted as a Sound guard ship, beginning service there on 27 September 1917 under the Commander of Security of the Middle Baltic, and replacing the older battleship *Lothringen*. There were no special events or incidents during this time. During the period of unrest and revolution, *Hannover* remained loyal to the Kaiser and on 11 November 1918 went to Swinemünde, from where she returned to Kiel on 14–15 November in company with *Schlesien*. She was decommissioned on 17 December 1918.

Pommern

Namesake: Prussian province on the Baltic.

The third ship of the *Deutschland* class was laid on the cradle of the builder's dockyard on 22 March 1904. Owing to extremely low water, the launching had to be delayed from the foreseen 19 November 1905 until 2 December. *Pommern* was transferred to Kiel dockyard in early July 1907, where after the installation of the heavy artillery the trials commenced on 6 August 1907. With a speed of 18.7 knots, *Pommern* was the fastest pre-dreadnought battleship in the world at this time. *Pommern* was completed with supplemental oil firing, and on 11 November 1907 she joined II Squadron.

From 1908 to 1914, *Pommern* took part in all the cruises, exercises and manoeuvres of the fleet, interrupted by periods in the dockyard and, in 1909 and 1912, by icing in the Baltic. After the beginning of World War I, *Pommern* also took part in all the operations conducted by II Squadron, and so it was that she came to the Skagerrak battle on 31 May 1916.

Towards 0300hrs on 1 June, II Squadron came into contact with the British 12th Destroyer Flotilla. The battleships turned away to starboard to avoid torpedoes, but at 0310hrs *Pommern* was struck by one, or perhaps two, torpedoes fired by the destroyer *Onslaught*. A series of powerful explosions

B

DESTRUCTION OF SMS *POMMERN*

In early 1915, the Imperial Navy undertook measures to improve the underwater protection of its pre-dreadnought ships against mine and torpedo attacks. These vessels did not have the carefully developed and extremely effective underwater protection systems integrated into the construction of the dreadnought capital ships. Instead, the measures consisted mainly of moving or deleting the shells and powder cartridges located in the outboard chambers (magazines) and filling the voids with empty wooden boxes. The utility of these measures was invalidated in October 1915, when the armoured cruiser *Prinz Adalbert* was torpedoed by a submarine and exploded and sank.

At the beginning of the war, Vizeadmiral Scheer was chief of II Squadron. Whether this meant he was more sympathetic to the pleas of later II Squadron chief Konteradmiral Mauve, who wanted to accompany the High Sea Fleet on the operation of 31 May 1916, remains unknown. During the Skagerrak battle, II Squadron provided excellent service in fending off an attack by British battlecruisers on I AG (Reconnaissance Group) at 2130hrs in the evening. The following day at 0310hrs, in the early morning half-light, *Pommern* was struck by one or two torpedoes. A series of explosions followed briefly and flames spread over the entire ship, reaching mast high. *Pommern* broke in two and pieces of debris whirled through the air, as *Hannover* sheered out to starboard to avoid the floating wreck. *Pommern* had fallen victim to a torpedo from the destroyer *Onslaught*.

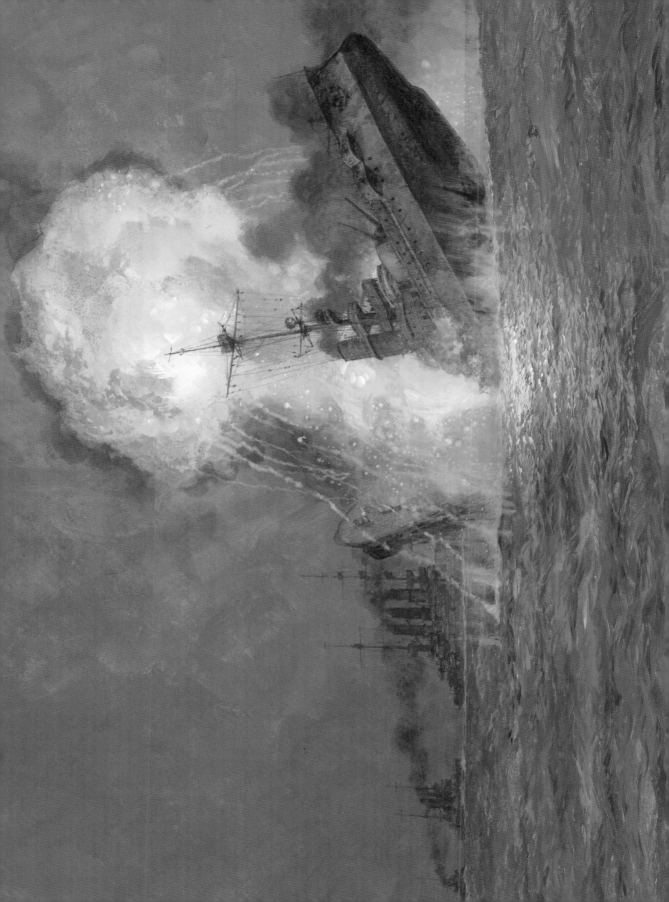

The battleship *Pommern*, seen here before the war, was lost with all hands in the Skaggerak battle, on the morning of 1 June 1914.

followed one another at brief intervals – it was later thought that a 17cm magazine had detonated. From starboard, flames spread over the entire ship and reached past the mastheads. *Pommern* eventually broke in two; the next ship astern, *Hannover*, had to sheer out of line to starboard to avoid the floating stern half of the ship, on which the propellers and rudder towered high into the air. The entire crew of 839 officers and men perished.

The loss of *Pommern* shows that the provisional measures taken to improve the underwater protection of these ships, such as moving munitions inboard, were ineffective and that they were inadequately protected against modern torpedoes and mines.

Schlesien
Namesake: Prussian province.

The contracts for the last two ships of the *Deutschland* class, *Schlesien* and *Schleswig-Holstein*, were awarded by the RMA on 11 June 1904. On 19 November, the dockyard of F. Schichau in Danzig struck the keel for *Schlesien*. Launching followed on 28 May 1906, and in March 1908 *Schlesien* steamed to Kiel for final fitting out, where she was commissioned on 5 May 1908. The trials were interrupted when *Schlesien* was made a torpedo trials ship from 6 July to 5 September 1908. After this duty was completed, she joined I Squadron and began the usual service in the High Sea Fleet, taking part in the normal unit and fleet manoeuvres. In April 1910, she transferred to Wilhelmshaven as part of I Squadron, but after being transferred to II Squadron on 3 November 1911, Kiel again became her home port. In 1914 she began the war with this squadron.

From August 1914, *Schlesien* carried out picket and security duty in the German Bight, and took part in the fleet operations on 15–16 December 1914, 17–18 April 1915, 21–23 April 1915, 17–18 May and 23–24 October. In March 1916 she served briefly as a target for U-boat training in the Baltic, and then on 24–25 April 1916 participated in the fleet operation against the English coast.

On 31 May to 1 June 1916, *Schlesien* took part in the Skagerrak battle. During the action, splinters from a shell that landed short killed one man and wounded another. During the night march, *Schlesien* was engaged by British destroyers, but suffered no damage.

After this battle, service as a picket and security ship continued, interrupted again by service as a target ship for U-boats in June and July. From 31 January to 9 February 1917, *Schlesien* then served as a guard and ice rescue ship in the Sound. (The ships of this class were particularly well suited to icebreaking because of the shape of their ram bows.) Further duty in the picket service followed from 2 May to 8 June 1917 and then she again served as a target ship in the Baltic. *Schlesien* finally quit the Elbe mouth position for good on 27 July 1917, and was then retired from II Squadron. From 20 August 1917 to 16 April 1918, she served as a recruit and stoker training ship in the Baltic. At the end of April, *Schlesien* went to the Imperial Dockyard in Kiel and was converted to a sea cadet school ship. Meanwhile, from 17 August to

23 September, the heavy and medium artillery was removed and replaced by guns of 10.5cm and 8.8cm calibre. Several training cruises were undertaken before revolutionary unrest broke out in Kiel. Therefore on 5 November 1918, under the Imperial battle flag and under threat from those flying the red banner, *Schlesien* departed Kiel. At first she went to Flensburg, and then Arö. On instructions from the RMA, she then sailed to Swinemünde, arriving there on 9 November, where her commander lowered his flag the following day. Nevertheless, Fregattenkapitän von Waldeyer-Hartz remained onboard with a reduced crew, and on 14 November *Schlesien* began the journey back to Kiel, with her engines and boilers being served by cadets. She arrived on 15 November and was decommissioned on 1 December 1918.

The aft deck of *Schlesien* during the war. Whilst some officers rest atop the aft turret, one having brought his wicker chair, some men drill on deck.

Schleswig-Holstein

Namesake: The Prussian province taken in the war of 1867.

For some unknown reason, the Germania Dockyard, Kiel, took 14 months to begin construction of *Schleswig-Holstein* – having received the contract on 11 June 1904 the keel was not struck until 18 August 1905, therefore being the last pre-dreadnought battleship of the Imperial Navy. After being launched on 17 December 1906, *Schleswig-Holstein* was commissioned on 6 July 1908, the staff having come from sistership *Schlesien*. Following the conclusion of trials, she joined II Squadron on 21 September 1908. The usual training, manoeuvres and foreign cruises followed.

As with the other vessels of II Squadron, *Schleswig-Holstein* carried out picket and security duties after the outbreak of war, before the fleet operation of 15–16 December 1914 and other missions in 1915 and 1916. In April she demounted two 8.8cm cannon and replaced them with two BAK guns of the same calibre.

The last great operation for the ship was the Skagerrak battle. During the evening of 31 May, II Squadron came into contact with the British battlecruisers. At 2132hrs a large-calibre shell struck the VI casemate of *Schleswig-Holstein*. A 17cm gun and the starboard signal position was hit and three men were killed and eight were wounded. During the night march on 1 June, there was further contact with British destroyers at around 0300hrs and these were engaged by the ships of II Squadron. Damage repairs took place from 10 June to 25 June 1916. After that the ship served as a target ship for U-boats and from 12 to 23 February 1917 interrupted this duty with service in the Sound watch. In the spring of 1917, *Schleswig-Holstein* went to Altenbruch where she was decommissioned on 2 May 1917. She was mainly disarmed and was assigned to the 5th U-boat Flotilla, which was formed on 10 September 1917, as an accommodation ship in Bremerhaven. From 1918 she lay in Kiel, where she remained until the end of the war.

THE FIRST DREADNOUGHT TYPE

The construction of the British battleship *Dreadnought* took the naval world by surprise. The cause of the shock was not so much that she was the first all-big-gun ship completed, as this had been discussed and planned for some time – the American *Michigan* class vessels were designed before *Dreadnought* – nor because she was a quantum leap in size – she was actually just 10 per

Schlesien tied up in the Imperial Dockyard, Kiel, during the war. In the background is the transporter bridge at the entrance to the dockyard.

cent larger than her predecessor – but because of the remarkably short time in which she was constructed. *Dreadnought* was laid down on 2 October 1905, was launched on 10 February 1906, and was ready to undertake trials on 3 October 1906, just one year and one day after being laid down. Apart from the excellent work performed by Portsmouth Naval Dockyard, the reasons for this rapid construction were the pre-ordering and prefabrication of materials and the utilization of 12in gun turrets built for the *Lord Nelson* class, even though this meant delay in the completion of these ships.

In foreign navies, the trend for battleships was towards having a medium-calibre battery to supplement the main calibre armament. This trend began with the Italian battleship *Regina Margherita* of 1900, which carried 4 x 12in cannon and 4 x 8in medium-calibre guns. Although other foreign navies immediately followed this trend, the German Imperial Navy did not. The first advocate for a battleship armed with artillery of a large uniform calibre was the British officer Admiral John Fisher, who promoted this idea in 1900. Then in 1903 the notable Italian designer Vittorio Cuniberti published the plans for his 'ideal battleship for the Royal Navy', armed with 12 x 12in quick-firing guns. This design suggested a uniform large number of guns and also a speed that was completely out of the question for battleships at the time.

Meanwhile, on 9 December 1903 the Kaiser asked the Development Department of the RMA to develop a battleship of 13,000 tonnes with 4 x 28cm and 4 x 21cm cannon. It was the first step to increasing the size and armament of the German battleships, which generally were smaller and less powerfully armed than their foreign contemporaries. The reasons for this were twofold: Admiral Tirpitz did not want to appear as an aggressor and, secondly, smaller ships were cheaper. By the end of January 1904, three design studies were ready. Two of them had 21cm guns in four wing turrets, making a hexagonal arrangement with the 2 x 28cm turrets. This configuration remained unchanged throughout all subsequent German design projects. In March 1904, a memorandum by the General Navy Department (A) confirmed that a uniform increase in the medium gun calibre was desirable, rather than introducing a medium-calibre armament of two different calibres. The Department stated that two medium calibres would cause difficulties for fire control, theoretical training and the ammunition use. The international shipbuilding scene of 1904 showed many variations of the medium-calibre armament and the German design of 16 x 21cm cannon, including eight guns in double turrets, appeared justifiable in light of ships from other nations.

Just a few days after this design was presented, on 2 April 1904, the Construction Department (K) of the RMA addressed a memorandum to State Secretary Admiral Tirpitz demanding an all-big-gun battleship with no medium-calibre armament. This far-sighted document stated that the battleship must be capable of weakening the enemy, but must take into account the German special conditions, such as geographical disadvantage and financial constraints. The Construction Department listed many technical premises, such as numerous and well-protected decisive weapons, sufficient buoyancy, secure artillery direction, sufficient speed, good turning ability and an action radius appropriate to conditions. A fundamental difference between the views of the Construction Department and the General Navy Department was that the former thought an engagement

An aerial view of *Nassau* with turrets trained as the designers had envisaged – to port and starboard ahead. Unfortunately, by World War I an advance towards the enemy in this manner was tactically unsound.

would be fought at long range, therefore requiring a greater number of heavier cannon of at least 28cm calibre, whereas the latter expected the engagement to develop quickly into a short-range encounter, a view supported by Admiral Tirpitz until as late as 1910.

A meeting at the end of April brought the first crystallization of the new type, a 14,000–15,000-tonne ship with a 21cm medium-calibre outfit to support the four main 28cm guns. Admiral Tirpitz was against any further increase in size on economic and political grounds. On this basis, the Construction Department began work on two new projects.

In January and February 1905, the rumours concerning the size increase of future English battleships seemed to be confirmed, and a displacement of 18,000 tonnes was expected for the *Nelson* class. Therefore, on 20 February Admiral Tirpitz requested two more development studies, one with 21cm medium guns and six double turrets, and the other with 8 x 28cm SK quick-firing guns, but still of around 15,000 tonnes. At a meeting on 18 March 1905, further increases in size were agreed to and the designs, including two all-big-gun 28cm gun drafts, were submitted to the Kaiser. Wilhelm II approved an all-big-gun design, which had 8 x 28cm guns arranged in two double and four single turrets in a hexagon layout. The decision had been taken, and a design with medium-calibre guns was never again considered.

The new project, known as 'G', followed in September 1905, with a further displacement increase to 18,400 tonnes, and was approved by the Kaiser on 4 October. Project G7b, approved by the Kaiser on 3 March 1906, was the immediate predecessor of the *Nassau* class. The armament now consisted of 12 x 28cm cannon in a hexagonal arrangement, and there were three funnels. Refinement of this design led to two funnels so that space was better utilized, and towing tests suggested a speed of 19½ knots could be obtained with 22,000 indicated horsepower (ihp).

On 26 March 1906, the Reichstag finally authorized the new budget, which included the necessary funds for the first two German dreadnought battleships. Five days later, on 31 March 1906, the order for the first of the new ships, *Nassau*, was placed with the Imperial Dockyard, Wilhelmshaven. The jump from *Deutschland* to *Nassau* represented a much greater leap than the British made with *Dreadnought*. Whilst *Dreadnought* was 10 per cent bigger than her predecessor, *Nassau* was 43 per cent larger than *Deutschland* and cost 37.399 million marks compared to 24.481 million marks. The artillery outfit was tripled from 4 x 28cm guns to 12 x 28cm cannon. Nevertheless, many of the infrastructure changes to facilitate the great length and, more importantly, the greater beam of the new ships had already been undertaken. In 1901 work was undertaken in Wilhelmshaven to enlarge Slipway 2, build three new dry docks (Nos 4, 5 and 6) and to construct the

ABOVE

Hannover on watch in the Sound with anti-torpedo nets deployed.

ABOVE RIGHT

Nassau and *Westfalen* at the opening of III Entrance to Wilhelmshaven Dockyard, 15 October 1909

new lock, Entrance III. All these things would be finished by 1909. However, enlargement of the Kaiser Wilhelm Canal was only begun in 1907.

The design of the new capital ships was entrusted to the Geheime Oberbaurat (Secret Designer), Hans Bürkner. In his memoirs he wrote that Admiral Tirpitz wanted to avoid creating a confrontational situation with the English and instead wanted to increase the quality of German ships. Initially, German design had roughly followed the English model, but the designers were gradually developing their own design philosophies. In particular, the heavy damage to the battleship *Kaiser Friedrich III*, which grounded on Adlersgrund during the night of 1–2 April 1900, led to watertight bulkheads and a powerful drainage system. The importance of these design concepts was confirmed by the events of the Russo-Japanese War (1904–05), when many battleships were destroyed or damaged by underwater weapons. Therefore, the new capital ships required the optimum underwater protective systems and Tirpitz attached great importance to this goal, ordering large-scale trials and making substantial funds available.

Great Britain and Italy had carried out torpedo tests on old ships, but the tests were not conducted systematically and could not be evaluated. The Imperial Navy, therefore, decided to construct a special test target, which was about 20m long and represented the middle part of a ship. It was divided into a 10m-long centre section and two short end compartments, closed above by an armoured deck, and weighed around 1,500 tonnes. The target was supported by a float that was 36m long and was filled with empty barrels. This test rig was used to perfect the development of the armoured torpedo bulkhead protection system, and trials were conducted from 1906 to 1914. After each test, the target was rebuilt with appropriate changes to the defensive characteristics, and the explosive charges were progressively increased. It was found that the effectiveness of the torpedo bulkhead varied according to its distance from the outer skin and its thickness. It was also discovered that coal stored in the protective bunker had a substantial defensive quality.

Trials were also conducted to test the effectiveness of torpedo nets. Although the nets meant the explosion was kept away from the hull and the large hole in the outer skin was avoided, there was distortion over a greater area. The building officials were against the use of these nets, while the serving officers of the RMA advocated their reintroduction. There was an impasse that Tirpitz could solve only by introducing the nets 'as a trial'.

Of course, after the Skagerrak battle, when ships had to stop to clear away the damaged nets and prevent them fouling the propellers, the dangers of the nets became fully apparent and they were immediately removed.

Further trials used torpedo bulkheads of different types of steel, allowing thinner bulkheads to be employed. Yet other trials tested the security of ammunition and torpedo warheads against underwater hits, and the behaviour of fuel oil tanks. Trials intended to test the protective systems against the effect of an artillery shell hit beneath the waterline could not be undertaken. All of these scenarios were duly played out in reality during the war.

Sailors perform rifle drill on *Nassau*'s forecastle. It is evident that correct footwear was not essential in the Imperial Navy.

The results of these trials and the development of underwater protection in the Imperial Navy were that during World War I the German ships' defensive capabilities were far superior to those of any other navy, a point which was tried and proven on many occasions. The German ships' wider beams were therefore a product of defensive criteria, but this also allowed them to carry heavier artillery and had the advantage that the ships were almost unsinkable.

BATTLESHIPS OF THE *NASSAU* CLASS

After the Reichstag gave approval for the first four ships of the new type at the end of March 1906, and gave funds for the first two, the following building contracts were let: *Nassau* to the Imperial Dockyard, Wilhelmshaven; *Westfalen* to A.G. Weser, Bremen; *Posen* to the Germania Dockyard, Kiel; and *Rheinland* to A.G. Vulcan, Stettin. There was then a break of around seven to ten months, however, before building began because of the need to purchase arms and armour. As with *Dreadnought*, the German ships were built under conditions of strict secrecy and at accelerated speed. For example, *Nassau* was constructed and launched in just seven and a half months, and fitting out was completed in 19 months. It was naval policy in Germany for various private yards to participate in the construction programme, so that no one yard had a monopoly and therefore prices would be kept competitive. The privately constructed yards took only 27, 35 and 36 months to build *Nassau*'s sisterships.

Nassau was slightly (around 700 tonnes) heavier than *Dreadnought* and the weight distribution of the two ships was as follows:

	Weight as percentage of displacement (tonnes)	
	Nassau	*Dreadnought*
Hull and structure	36.7	37.7
Armour	36.0	28.0
Machinery	8.0	11.4
Armament	13.0	17.3
Construction and building reserve	1.2	0.6
Normal fuel	5.1	5.0

With *Dreadnought* the proportions for armament and machinery were greater, but armour was lower. The lack of a building reserve meant than when completed the extra weights incurred during building caused the ship to sit deeper than planned.

	Nassau	Westfalen	Rheinland	Posen
Building dockyard	Imperial, Wilhelmshaven	A.G. Weser, Bremen	A.G. Vulcan, Stettin	Germania, Kiel
Contract	31 May 1906	30 October 1906	16 November 1906	13 November 1906
Building number	30	163	287	132
Keel laying	22 July 1907	12 August 1907	1 June 1907	11 June 1907
Launched	7 March 1908	1 July 1908	26 September 1908	12 December 1908
Commissioned	1 October 1909	16 November 1909	30 April 1910	31 May 1910
Displacement (tonnes)	Designed: 18,873 Loaded: 20,535	Designed: 18,873 Loaded: 20,535	Designed: 18,873 Loaded: 20,535	Designed: 18,873 Loaded: 20,535
Length (metres)	146.1	146.1	146.1	146.1
Beam (metres)	26.9	26.9	26.9	26.9
Draught (metres)	Construction: 8.57 Loaded: 8.76	Construction: 8.57 Loaded: 8.76	Construction: 8.57 Loaded: 8.76	Construction: 8.57 Loaded: 8.76
Moulded depth (metres)*	13.25	13.25	13.25	13.25
Performance (indicated horsepower)	Designed 22,000 Maximum 26,244	Designed 22,000 Maximum 26,792	Designed 22,000 Maximum 27,498	Designed 22,000 Maximum 28,117
Revolutions per minute	124	121	123	123
Speed (knots)	Designed: 19.0 Maximum: 20.06	Designed: 19.0 Maximum: 20.3	Designed: 19.0 Maximum: 20.03	Designed: 19.0 Maximum: 20.13
Fuel (tonnes) – fuel oil from 1915	Construction: 950 Maximum: 2,700 160 tonnes oil	Construction: 950 Maximum: 2,700 160 tonnes oil	Construction: 950 Maximum: 2,700 160 tonnes oil	Construction: 950 Maximum: 2,700 160 tonnes oil
Range (nautical miles)	8,100nm at 10 knots 8,300nm at 12 knots	8,100nm at 10 knots 8,300nm at 12 knots	8,100nm at 10 knots 8,300nm at 12 knots	9,400nm at 10 knots 8,300nm at 12 knots
Cost (millions of gold marks)	37.399	37.615	36.916	36.920
Compartments	16	19	19	19
Double Bottom (as percentage of length)	88	88	88	88
Crew	40 officers 968 men	40 officers 968 men	40 officers 968 men	40 officers 968 men

*Moulded depth is the vertical distance from the keel to the uppermost deck, taken inside the ship's plating

Armament

The armament of this class has been the cause of much debate, then and now. It consisted of 12 x 28cm SK L/45 cannon mounted in a hexagonal arrangement. The reasons offered for this arrangement reveal many contradictions. At first it was suggested that it allowed 'fire to two sides' as the battleships 'advanced against the enemy line and in the following mêlée.' The concept of an all-out mêlée was quite obsolete by the time the *Nassau* class was designed, but a further reason offered was having a reserve of turrets in the fire lee. Yet owing to the high angles of descent of long-range shellfire, the lee turrets were just as exposed as those on the engaged side, and the idea of a battle line reversing course to bring its reserve turrets into action is tactical nonsense. Nevertheless, the hexagonal arrangement did offer structural advantages and allowed a shorter ship length.

The choice of 28cm calibre was more obvious. The new German 28cm L/45 was scarcely inferior to the English 12in QF L/45 Mk X in performance and had a high rate of fire of three projectiles per minute. In any case, the German 30.5cm cannon was not then available. In the previous battleships, there had been one continuous elevator from the magazines to the turrets. With the new class this changed. Because the wing turrets were close to the ship's side, old-style elevators would have been outside the protective torpedo bulkhead, therefore the elevators were fitted inside the torpedo bulkhead and went only as far as a turntable, or working chamber. From there an elevator that rotated with the turret took the munitions up to the guns. *Nassau* and *Westfalen* had this type of elevator for all their turrets, the 28cm L/45 Drh.L C/06 turntable, with a fixed lower elevator. On *Posen* and *Rheinland*, the Drh.L C/07 was employed for the forward and aft turrets. On this model the lower elevator was attached to the turntable and rotated with the turret. The turrets were also of a new design, the first to be fitted with built-in rangefinders. The cannon could be elevated from -6° to 20°, with a maximum range for the 302kg armour-piercing projectile of 189hm, which was improved to 204hm in 1915. An outfit of 900 28cm shells was carried. On *Nassau* and *Westfalen*, the fore and aft turrets had shell rooms on the upper platform deck and the munition chambers below them on the lower platform deck. The wing turrets and all the turrets of *Posen* and *Rheinland* had this order reversed, with the munition chambers above the shell rooms, and in the case of the wing turrets each chamber and room was located one deck lower, the shell rooms being on the Stauung, or hold.

Unlike her contemporaries *Dreadnought* and *Michigan*, which only carried a 7.6cm secondary armament, *Nassau* was fitted with a medium-calibre armament of 14 x 15cm guns, which were new model L/45 guns in MPL C/06 pivot mounts, these weapons replacing the 17cm cannon of the previous class. A total of 1,800 15cm shells were carried and the 45.3kg shells could reach a range of 135hm, and then 168hm after 1915, travelling at a high velocity of 835mps. The *Nassau* class also mounted a battery of 16 x 8.8cm torpedo-boat/destroyer defence guns. A total of 2,400 rounds were carried and the shells weighed 9.5kg. These guns were already becoming too light to deal effectively with the ever-larger destroyers and in 1915 two of them were replaced with the excellent 8.8cm Flak (anti-aircraft) L/45 C/13 cannon.

The ships of the *Nassau* class were fitted with a total of 6 x 45cm underwater torpedo tubes. There was a bow and a stern tube, and two on each broadside, mounted ahead and astern of the citadel. Such a number of tubes shows that the design philosophy was still orientated towards a close-range battle. The C/07 torpedo weighed 800kg with a warhead of 110kg. A total of 16 torpedoes were carried and they had a range of just 2,000m at 32 knots, or 1,500m at 36 knots.

Damage to the bow of *Nassau* after the collision with the British destroyer *Spitfire* during the Skagerrak battle.

Nassau heeled over to port during trimming tests.

Class for class, the German dreadnought battleships had thicker armour distributed over a wider area than their British contemporaries, as this image shows (measurements in millimetres). This was also the case with all subsequent classes. *Dreadnought* had a very narrow belt which quickly reduced in thickness. *Westfalen* had a thicker belt, over a wider area, which gradually tapered towards the upper and lower edges. The German ship had torpedo bulkhead protection against underwater weapons, totally absent on *Dreadnought* and subsequent British designs.

Armour

When compared with the preceding class the armour was much stronger. The percentage of weight allocated to armour was 36%. The armoured belt extended far forward and aft which improved the protection of the ships' ends and would prevent large holes and the accompanying great inrush of water, the so-called "barn door" effect. On *Nassau* the main belt was 270mm, and with her sisterships 290mm thick. This was reduced to 80mm far forward and 90mm aft. In German literature it is normal to refer to the main belt as the belt, and the upper belt as citadel armour. The upper belt over the casemates was 160mm. In all German ships the citadel and belt extended over a much larger area than in foreign navies. The main belt and citadel were closed by two transverse armoured bulkheads of 200mm thickness. Because of the belief that battle ranges would quickly reduce, the deck armour was not as thick as it could have been. The upper deck above the casemates was 25mm thick and the armoured deck was 38mm. The sloping armoured deck, or Böschung was 58mm. The barbettes' and turrets' faces were 280mm, the turret sides 220mm thick. The sloping turret roof was 90mm, and the flat roof 60mm. The forward conning tower was very well protected with 400mm thickness, the aft conning tower was 200mm. The citadel area was protected by an armoured torpedo bulkhead of 20mm thickness. The armour was Krupp cemented steel.

Seakeeping

Nassau had a metacentric height of 2.33m. Compared to *Deutschland*, which had a lower metacentric height of 0.95m, the mass moment of inertia was moved substantially upwards by the higher weights, producing a faster and more violent roll. Therefore bilge keels were subsequently fitted to prevent rolling. Nevertheless, they were moderate sea ships which manoeuvred well, having a small turning circle.

Machinery

It is often said amongst maritime historians that the

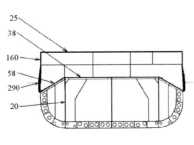

Westfalen

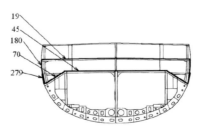

Dreadnought

hexagonal turret arrangement of the *Nassau* and *Helgoland* classes was due to the large space requirements for the piston engines. This opinion is incorrect. Of the two American ships of the *Delaware* class, *Delaware* had reciprocating engines and *North Dakota* had turbines, with no noticeable difference between the ships. The extra height required with piston engines was not an issue for battleships. The reason for fitting reciprocating engines was that turbine manufacture in Germany was not yet ready for large-scale production. Therefore the *Nassau* class were fitted with three, three-cylinder triple-expansion engines. The wider beam meant that the three engine rooms were adjacent to one another. Each engine drove a 5m diameter propeller.

There were 12 naval boilers arranged in three divided boiler rooms. From the winter of 1915, the coal-fired boilers were provided with supplemental oil firing. Two rudders were fitted in parallel and were powered by steam rudder engines. There were eight turbo-dynamos with a total output of 1,280kW at 225 volts. The drainage system of the *Nassau* class was of the so-called 'ring system': two large-diameter pipes ran down each side of the ship and were interconnected athwartships. Several groups of powerful drainage pumps served this system.

A close up of *Nassau's* 'C' turret and starboard side. The fitting of the derrick winch motor externally makes *Nassau* easy to recognize.

General characteristics and changes

Nassau differed from the others in that the gooseneck cranes were fitted with their electric drive motors externally. As completed *Nassau* and *Westfalen* had two large wireless antenna spreaders fitted to each mast. *Nassau's* were removed in 1911 and those of *Westfalen* in 1915. Spotting tops were fitted to the foremasts in 1914 and from 1915 the aft compass posts were removed. As with all ships, the torpedo nets were removed in 1916 after the Skagerrak battle.

Service record

Nassau

Namesake: German Duchy, from 1866 part of the Prussian province Hessen-Nassau.

Nassau's keel was struck on 22 July 1907, and launching followed after a relatively short period of time on 7 March 1908. However, while fitting out an unfortunate accident occurred. A dockyard worker inadvertently removed a blanking plate of a 45cm diameter pipe and water under powerful pressure flooded into the ship. The watertight bulkheads were not yet in place so that the lower parts of the ship filled and the ship sank 1.6m to rest on the bottom with a port list. The water was pumped out and the ship was moved to Dock IV, but removing the mud and silt was extremely difficult, incurring a delay.

A good close-up of *Nassau* anchored on the Wilhelmshaven Road on 10 August 1910.

Trials began on 1 October 1909 and were extended. On 16 October 1909, *Nassau* and *Westfalen* participated in the opening of

Nassau in a lock of III Entrance to Wilhelmshaven.

the new III Entrance, the large new lock for Wilhelmshaven Naval Dockyard. Although still on trials, these two battleships took part in the High Sea Fleet manoeuvres in February 1910. On 3 May, *Nassau* concluded her trials and I Squadron was formed. Prior to World War I, *Nassau* participated in all the normal training exercises and cruises.

During the war, *Nassau* was involved in the various fleet operations, interrupted only by dockyard and repair periods. In July 1915, supplemental oil firing was fitted. The following August, *Nassau* was part of I Squadron's advance into the Riga Gulf in the Baltic. She advanced with torpedo nets deployed and fired on the Russian battleship *Slava*. After the Russians retreated from the entrance to the Riga Gulf, *Nassau*, together with her sistership *Posen*, penetrated the Gulf on 19 August and remained there until 21 August. During this time, *Nassau* assisted in the destruction of the Russian gunboats *Sivuch* and *Koreets*.

On 31 May to 1 June 1916, *Nassau* took part in the Skagerrak battle. On the return journey she came into contact with British destroyers and had to avoid several torpedoes. At about 0030hrs *Nassau* was hit by two light-calibre shells that killed 11 men and wounded 16 others. Then she rammed the destroyer *Spitfire*, and consequently the upper hull was rent open for a length of 3.5m and the upper deck was damaged. Two shells fired from the forward turret passed through the destroyer's bridge without exploding, but gas pressure caused a great deal of damage. *Nassau* lost contact with the main body and only rejoined II Squadron at 0220hrs. She was under repair until 10 July 1916.

Nassau took part in the fleet advances in August and October 1916, then on 21 December she grounded in the mouth of the Elbe, but was able to get free under her own power. She was under repair in the Reihersteig Dockyard in Hamburg until 1 February 1917.

Nassau was involved in the fleet advance on 23–25 April 1918, although without any notable incidents, but in summer 1918 she was one of the ships allocated to Operation *Schlußstein* (Keystone), the plan to occupy St Petersburg. Therefore on 8 August she took aboard 250 Army troops in Wilhelmshaven, together with their equipment. From there she transferred to Kiel, but the operation was postponed and eventually cancelled, and on 22 August 1918 she returned to the North Sea. She stood ready for the planned operation at the end of October.

C SMS *WESTFALEN*

The first class of German dreadnoughts represented a quantum leap in size and carried three times the heavy armament of their predecessors. Six turrets in a hexagonal arrangement were a feature of every German design proposal, and it seems no other turret arrangement was considered. This fixation is interesting because the very first dreadnought design, the American *Michigan*, incorporated the superfiring arrangement that was to become the standard for capital ships. It was only because the US Congress delayed passing the appropriations bill that the *Michigan* class was not built before *Dreadnought*. Although the *Nassau* class had the hexagonal arrangement and thereby wasted one-third of the armament, the broadside still numbered eight heavy barrels.

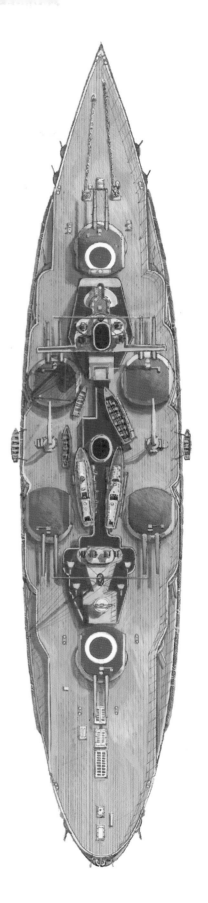

ABOVE
Nassau tied up on the southern quay in Wilhelmshaven, with Wilhelmshaven Roadstead beyond.

ABOVE RIGHT
Nassau being attended by the Lifting Crane I, more popularly known as 'Long Heinrich', which had a lifting capacity of 250 tonnes.

Nassau was not one of the ships interned at Scapa Flow, but, after the Germans scuttled those vessels, she was demanded as a replacement by the Entente and was awarded to Japan. She was sold to an English company and was wrecked at Dordrecht in 1920.

Westfalen

Namesake: Prussian province.

The keel for the battleship *Westfalen* was struck at A.G. Weser in Bremen on 12 August 1907, and on 1 July 1908 the ship was launched from the cradle. In mid-September 1909, the fitting-out work had progressed so far that *Westfalen* could be transferred to Wilhelmshaven for final fitting out, with a dockyard crew. At this time of year, the River Weser was so low that six pontoons had to be fitted to the hull to reduce the draught, but it was only with the second attempt that the ship was successfully transferred. *Westfalen* took part in the opening ceremonies for the new III Entrance. On 16 November 1909, she was commissioned and trials began, but these were interrupted when the ship took part in the fleet manoeuvres in February 1910. Trials continued until 3 May 1910, when *Westfalen* joined I Squadron, and on 5 May 1910 she became flagship of the squadron chief, who transferred his flag from *Hannover*. For the autumn of 1914, it was planned that *Westfalen* would go to II Squadron, but with the outbreak of war this plan came to nothing.

After the outbreak of war, *Westfalen* participated in all the major operations of I Squadron from 1914 to 1916, except the fleet advance of 29–30 March 1915, when she was in the dockyard. In August 1915, she participated in the attack on the Riga Gulf in the Baltic and supported the break-in to the Gulf by her sisterships.

In 1916 *Westfalen* took part in the Skagerrak battle and was particularly active during the night engagement. With the rear march, *Westfalen* became lead ship of the entire line and was especially active fending off the attacks by British destroyers. She was hit twice by medium-calibre shells and suffered two dead. On the next operation, on 19 August, she was the last ship in line when at 0600hrs, located 55 nautical miles north of Terschelling, she was hit by a torpedo fired by the British submarine E23. *Westfalen* took on 800 tonnes of water, but the anti-torpedo bulkhead saved her. Under the escort of three torpedo boats, she headed back to the German Bight and maintained a speed of 14 knots. Dockyard repairs were completed on 26 September 1916 and *Westfalen* went to the Baltic for training, before returning to the North Sea on 4 October so that she could participate in the fleet advance to the Dogger Bank on 19–20 October.

During 1917 there were no special events to report. During the Ösel operation she lay off Apenrade from 23 September to 20 October 1917 to oppose any attempted intervention by the British fleet, although none was forthcoming.

On 21 February 1918, *Westfalen* was made flagship of the 'Special Unit' under the command of Konteradmiral Meurer, formed to liberate Finland from Russia and communist forces. Therefore *Westfalen* was associated with an operation by the Imperial Navy that still has a positive result today. On 23 February, the Mecklenburg 14th Jäger Battalion was embarked aboard *Westfalen* and *Rheinland* and early the following morning they set off for Aland Island. The German plan was to occupy Aland as an advanced base, followed by the port of Hangö and finally the Finnish capital, Helsingfors. On 5 March, the unit reached Eckerö on Aland Island, despite encountering heavy winter ice. The Swedish had beaten them to the punch, however, and on the roads were the Swedish ships *Sverige*, *Oscar II* and *Thor*, supporting the Swedish troops ashore. After tense negotiations, the German troops landed on 7 March, and the first phase of the operation was over. *Westfalen* returned to Danzig.

Westfalen in the ice off Eckerö during the Finland operation in April 1918. In the background are the Swedish warships *Oscar II* and *Sverige*.

The second phase began on 31 March and on 3 April *Westfalen* and *Posen* arrived off Russarö, the outer defence of Hangö, which quickly fell. The third phase of the operation was the final move to occupy Helsingfors. On 9 April, *Westfalen* was off Reval collecting the invasion forces. On 11 April she passed the forts of the outer defences and anchored off Helsingfors, supporting the troops with her heavy artillery. By 14 April the operation was concluded and the communist forces had either surrendered or fled. *Westfalen* remained in Helsingfors until 30 April, by which time the objectives of the Navy had been fulfilled and the Svinhufuud government had been returned to power. *Westfalen* then returned to the North Sea.

Westfalen rejoined I Squadron and on 11 August 1918 took part in a fleet advance in the direction of Terschelling with the battleships *Kaiser*, *Kaiserin* and *Posen*, for the security of torpedo-boat forces. During the advance she suffered boiler damage that reduced her speed to 16 knots. She was subsequently retired from I Squadron and was assigned to the Ships Artillery Inspectorate as an Artillery School Ship.

Westfalen was not interned at the end of the war and remained in Kiel, where she was retired on 18 December 1918, stricken from the fleet list on 5 November 1919 and was delivered to Britain on 5 August 1920. She was wrecked in Birkenhead in 1924.

Rheinland

Namesake: Prussian-owned Rhine province.

The RMA assigned the building of the last ship of the class, *Rheinland*, to A.G. Vulcan in Stettin on 16 November 1906, and the keel was struck on 1 June 1907. The ship was launched on 26 September 1908.

D **SMS *RHEINLAND***

The battleship *Rheinland* participated in almost all the operations of I Squadron in the North Sea and Baltic. Most of *Rheinland*'s interior hull space was taken up with the 12 boilers, coal, three reciprocating engines, torpedo rooms and munition chambers and stores. The remaining space was used to accommodate the men forward, and officers aft. Like all German capital ships up until 1913 a closed ring drainage system was installed with leakage pumps forward and aft and, additionally, the condenser circulation pumps could be used with this system.

16   15   14   13   12   11   10   9

1. 110cm searchlights
2. Conning tower
3. 28cm turret A
4. Working chamber
5. Shell hoist
6. 8.8cm gun
7. Crew accommodation (not shown)
8. Shells
9. Magazine
10. 15cm medium-calibre gun
11. Boiler gas uptakes
12. Boiler room
13. Protective bunker
14. Wing passage
15. Transverse frame
16. Engine room

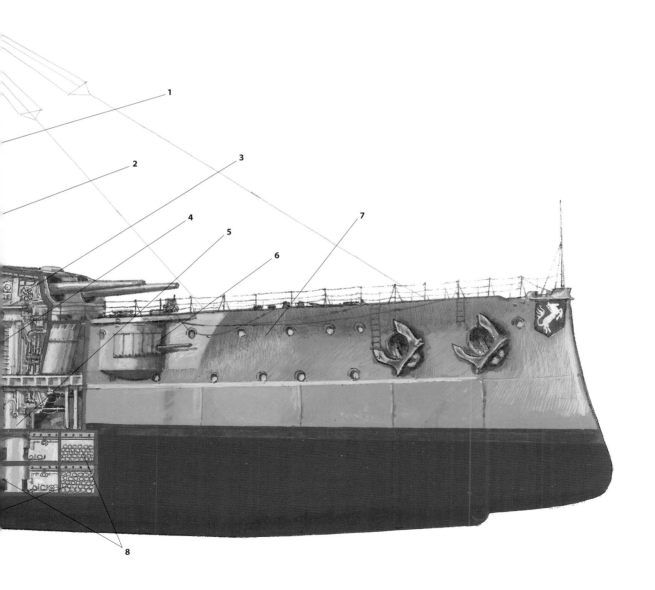

Torpedo strike on Westfalen

On 19 August 1916, Admiral Scheer led the High Sea Fleet across the North Sea to bombard the English coastal town of Sunderland. This was the operation that had originally been planned for 31 May, but which had been postponed, and the replacement undertaking led to the Skagerrak battle. Of course, the military value of such a bombardment was little – it was merely a provocation that was intended to lure part of the British forces to sea to be overwhelmed. At 0611hrs, 55 nautical miles north of Terschelling, the last ship in the German line, *Westfalen*, was struck by a torpedo launched by the English submarine E23. The resulting damage gives an excellent illustration of the defensive qualities of the German torpedo protection system, which had been meticulously developed for the new dreadnought-type battleships.

The torpedo struck the starboard hull side amidships, at frame 53 approximately 5m below the waterline. The outer protective coal bunker, and the inboard boiler room bunker were full of coal. It was German policy to use coal from outlying bunkers first during such operations, and save coal near the boilers for the action and to preserve its protective effect. The double hull side and wing passage were void. The detonation of the torpedo tore a large hole in the outer skin and wing passage bulkhead. Both were rent and badly bent inboard. However, the protective armoured torpedo bulkhead held firm and was practically undamaged. In the area of the explosion it was slightly bowed inwards, to a maximum of 160mm, some rivets were loosened

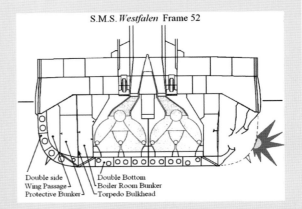

S.M.S. *Westfalen* Frame 52

Double side Wing Passage Protective Bunker — Double Bottom — Boiler Room Bunker — Torpedo Bulkhead

and some interior reinforcing angles were bent. A protective bunker door leaked slightly, but there was no other leakage inside the torpedo bulkhead. Some double side cells filled with water along with the wing passage and protective bunkers of compartments VIII and IX and some double bottom cells, for a total of 800 tonnes of water in the ship. The draught forward increased from 8.6m to 9.0m and aft from 8.4m to 8.6m and the ship took a 5° list to starboard. No men were killed. *Westfalen* was detached back to Wilhelmshaven and maintained a speed of 14 knots.

The torpedo protection system had worked perfectly. The combination of the wing passage, protective coal and armoured torpedo bulkhead had prevented any serious internal damage to the ship, even though the torpedo had struck at the level of the bulkhead between the aft and middle boiler rooms. Flooding had been confined to the outer hull. The naval architects involved in the design and construction of *Westfalen* should have been justifiably proud.

Trials were undertaken in the Swinemünder Bight from 23 February to 4 March 1910 by a dockyard crew, and then she was transferred to Kiel and was commissioned on 30 April 1910. On 30 August the normal trials were completed and *Rheinland* steamed to Wilhelmshaven where the crew was reduced. The crew went to commission the new Panzerkreuzer (armoured cruiser) named *von der Tann*, which illustrates the perennial shortage of trained crew that affected the Imperial Navy. It was only after the conclusion of the autumn manoeuvres that the crew of *Rheinland* was filled on 21 September, using the crew of *Zähringen*, which was decommissioned. *Rheinland* now took her place in I Squadron and took part in the winter cruise of the fleet in October, and the fleet exercises in November.

In the pre-war period, *Rheinland* participated in all the fleet activities, including the summer cruises to Norway in 1911, 1913 and 1914. When war broke out, from August 1914 to April 1915 *Rheinland* similarly took part in all the advances of the fleet. During the advance to the Dogger Bank on

A view of *Westfalen* in the ice off Eckerö during the Finnish operation in April 1918. Konteradmiral Meuer had the foresight to bring an automobile, which can be seen on the ice aft of *Westfalen*, in which he toured the islands.

24 April, she suffered a break in the high-pressure cylinder of the starboard engine and was only repaired by 23 May. In August 1915, *Rheinland* took part in the operation to attack the Riga Gulf, without incident, and on 11–12 September and 23–24 October was involved in advances into the North Sea.

In early 1916, *Rheinland* went into the dockyard for an extended period of overhaul work, from 12 February to 19 April 1916, but undertook the advance on 21–22 April and supported the coastal raid on 24–25 April 1916. During the Skagerrak battle, *Rheinland* fought with British destroyers during the night and at 0036hrs on 1 June suffered two 6in-calibre shell hits on the forward funnel. These caused ten dead and 20 wounded. The damage was repaired at the Imperial Dockyard, Wilhelmshaven, from 1 June to 22 June 1916. On 18–22 August, the battleship was deployed in the fleet advance to the English coast, then covered a torpedo-boat advance on 25–26 September, before participating in a further fleet advance on 18–20 October.

In 1917, *Rheinland* undertook security and picket duty. There was unrest amongst the sailors because of poor food during July and August 1917. During the attack on the Baltic Islands, *Rheinland* was positioned in the western Baltic from 15 September to 20 October 1917, in order to be available should British forces attempt to break into the Baltic to help the Russians.

On 22 February 1918, *Rheinland* and *Westfalen* were assigned to the Special Unit for the Finnish operation. On 6 March, the battleship arrived on Eckerö Roads in the Aland Islands where her commander functioned as 'Senior Sea Commander' until 10 April. The battleships covered the landing of the Army troops and their required supplies. On 11 April, *Rheinland* quit Eckerö to join the unit at Helsingfors, after which she would return to Danzig to replenish her coal bunkers. At 0730hrs in fog, however, she ran aground on Lagskär Island at a speed of 15 knots. Two men perished. There was extensive damage to the inner skin and three boiler rooms were flooded. From 18 to 20 April, the 2nd Admiral of the Special Unit, Konteradmiral Hartog, attempted to get *Rheinland* free and refloat her, which proved impossible, as *Rheinland* was stuck fast on the rocky ledge for about two-thirds of her length. When it became obvious that recovery work would be long and arduous, on 26 April the crew was ordered from the ship to commission *Schlesien*. All non-fixed weights were removed and after a floating crane arrived from Danzig on 8 May, the citadel and bow armour was removed, followed by the guns and some of the turret armour. A total weight of 6,400 tonnes was removed from the ship. With the aid of pontoons attached to the sides of the hull, the battleship was finally refloated on 9 July and was towed to Mariehamn, where

Rheinland before the war. Pre-war German ships carried identification bands around their funnels, but these were painted over after the war began. However, ships could always be identified by their heraldic shields.

A sea-level view of *Rheinland* in the ice off Eckerö on Aland Island, April 1918.

some repair work was carried out. On 24 July, using her centre engine and under the tow of two tugs, she departed for Kiel, where she arrived on 27 July. The tow unit was escorted by *Nautilus* and picket boats. Means to perform the extensive repair work were not available at this time, and therefore on 4 October 1918 *Rheinland* was decommissioned and was used as an accommodation ship.

On 5 November 1919, *Rheinland* was stricken from the list of warships. The terms of the Armistice did not require her to be interned, but after the fleet was sunk in Scapa Flow she was among those ships demanded by the Allies. She was delivered to Dordrecht on 27 July 1920 and was sold by the Allies for scrapping.

Posen

Namesake: Prussian province.

The contract for the construction of *Posen* was awarded to the Germania Dockyard in Kiel and on 11 June 1907 the keel was struck. The ship was launched on 12 December 1908. Acceptance trials continued until the end of April 1910 and, after final fitting out at the Imperial Dockyard in Kiel, *Posen* was commissioned on 31 May 1910. The usual trials were completed on 27 August and on 7 September she arrived in Wilhelmshaven, where the crew was reduced. It was only with the decommissioning of *Wittelsbach* on 20 September that the crew of *Posen* reached its full establishment and she was officially incorporated into the High Sea Fleet. Thereafter she participated in manoeuvres and training for I Squadron.

During the war, *Posen* was employed as flagship of the 2nd Admiral of I Squadron and took part in all the fleet operations of 1914 and 1915, except that of 10–18 May 1915, when she was in dock for overhaul of her hull and propeller shafts.

On 4 August 1915, I Squadron was dispatched to the Baltic under the command of the previous chief of IV Squadron, Vizeadmiral Erhard Schmidt, to cover the break-in to the Riga Gulf. The attempt initially failed, however, as the mine defences in the entrance to the Gulf, the Irben Straits, were too strong to break though. For a continuation of the operation Vizeadmiral Schmidt demanded that the ships of IV Squadron, which had little resistance to underwater weapons, be replaced by more battleworthy units, and *Nassau* and *Posen* were substituted into the break-in unit. The Commander-in-Chief of the Baltic, Großadmiral Prinz Heinrich, concurred and on 13 August 1915 Vizeadmiral Schmidt embarked aboard *Posen* as his flagship.

On the afternoon of 16 August, *Posen* was in combat with the Russian battleship *Slava* and gunboat *Chrabry*, which guarded the Russian minefields. German minesweeping work continued under the cover of *Posen* and *Nassau* and at 0745hrs on 19 August German forces were able to force their way into the Riga Gulf. The battleships first advanced towards the Moon Sound and then steamed south towards Dünamünde and Riga. Here they intervened in an engagement that had developed between the cruiser *Augsburg* and the Russian gunboats *Sivuch* and *Koreets*. *Sivuch* was sunk by the heavy artillery of the battleships, and *Koreets* was so badly damaged that the following day she was abandoned and sunk. At around 1900hrs on 20 August, Schmidt quit the Riga Gulf and on 21 August lowered his flag on *Posen*. Later the same day, he disbanded the unit.

On 11 April 1918, *Rheinland* ran aground on Lagskär Island in fog. A total weight of 6,400 tonnes was removed before she was refloated on 9 July. This aerial photograph shows *Rheinland* with turrets and searchlights already removed.

On 27 August 1915, *Posen* returned to the North Sea and on 11–12 September 1915 took part in a fleet advance. Then on 4 March 1916, under the command of the 2nd Admiral aboard *Posen*, the *von der Tann*, *Nassau* and *Westfalen* advanced to Amrumbank to meet the auxiliary cruiser *Möwe* on her return home.

During the Skagerrak battle, *Posen* suffered no damage during the day action, but during a night attack by British destroyers at 0030hrs on 1 June *Posen* rammed the small cruiser *Elbing* as the cruiser passed across her bow to avoid torpedoes. *Posen* turned with hard rudder so there was only light contact, and although *Posen* suffered no damage, the cruiser was later sunk. At around 0110hrs, British destroyers approached from port. One was destroyed by *Posen* and another caught fire. *Posen* avoided two torpedoes and later fired upon another destroyer; the German battleship suffered no losses.

After a dockyard overhaul from 26 June to 17 July, *Posen* took part in the fleet advances of 18–20 August and 18–20 October. During 1917 she performed picket and security duties, and in July and August her crew was also in a state of unrest over poor living conditions. *Posen* did not participate in the Baltic Islands operation, but on 17 November 1917 she supported II AG in the battle against superior British forces.

In March 1918, *Posen* was assigned to the Special Unit for the Finnish operation. On 13–14 April, the Landing Corps of the ship took part in the occupation of Helsingfors, during which she suffered four dead and 12 wounded. From 18 to 20 April, the 2nd Admiral vainly attempted to free the grounded *Rheinland*. Then on 22 April, in Helsingfors harbour, *Posen* pushed onto an underwater wreck while anchoring and was detached from the Special Unit on 30 April. *Posen* entered the dock at the Imperial Dockyard, Kiel, from 3 to 5 May, where a damaged propeller blade was replaced.

On 2 October, *Posen* stood ready on the outer Jade River to cover the return of the Flanders-based U-boats, and likewise was ready for the proposed fleet advance at the end of that month. On 3 November, I Squadron ran into the mouth of the Elbe and on 9 November went to Wilhelmshaven. On 16 December 1918, the ship was officially decommissioned.

Posen did not belong to the unit of interned ships, but was stricken from the list of warships on 5 November 1919 and was allocated to Great Britain on 13 May 1920. The British sold her to Holland, where she was wrecked in 1922.

BATTLESHIPS OF THE *HELGOLAND* CLASS

In May 1906, the RMA received the first news that the British Admiralty had ordered the next series of battleships to be armed with 13.5in guns, equivalent to 34.3cm. This news came at a bad time for the RMA, as any cost increases would have to be approved by the Reichstag, and would result in two cost increase demands in quick succession. Because of the financial framework,

ABOVE LEFT
Rheinland and *Posen* in the North Sea. After their completion, it was necessary to fit bilge keels to the battleships of this class. Here they are handling the heavy swell very well.

ABOVE RIGHT
The battleship *Posen* before the war. *Posen* participated in almost all the wartime operations of the Fleet, giving stalwart service.

The winter of 1917–18 was particularly severe and this photograph shows *Posen* with Konteradmiral's flag in the Baltic.

it appeared doubtful in the winter of 1907–08 if any displacement increases could be made until the new Fleet Law Amendment in 1909–10. Yet because of the jump in cruiser size to the battlecruiser, among other things, the new cost increases would have to be brought forward to 1908 at the latest. The Navy was saved in this situation, however, by the premature dissolution of the Reichstag in December 1906, and therefore the debate over funding would not occur in an election year. Nevertheless, the amendment to the Naval Law was now planned for 1908. In the amendment, the replacement time for battleships was reduced from 25 years to 20 years, which meant that for the budget years of 1908 to 1911 three new battleships and one battlecruiser would be laid down annually, after which the numbers would reduce to two capital ships per annum. In reality, the RMA would have preferred to maintain an initial building rate of two battleships per year – first, to avoid adverse British reaction, and second, to avoid placing a strain on the Navy infrastructure. They had to follow what was enacted in Fleet Law, however, and also the Kaiser and public opinion were now firmly behind the increased building tempo.

Meanwhile, towards the end of 1906, the General Navy Department was advocating an increase in heavy artillery calibre to 30.5cm (12in), but otherwise to retain the basic design of the *Nassau* class with a small increase in displacement. An increase to 30.5cm calibre would enable actions to be fought at a longer range because of better armour-piercing performance, and would avoid a large calibre increase should the British adopt the 13.5in gun. In September 1906, the Construction Department delivered a design draft with 12 x 30.5cm cannon and a displacement of 22,000 to 23,100 tonnes, at a price of around 45 million gold marks. This design would require a new budget. Publicly, State Secretary Tirpitz was critical of the General Navy Department in this regard – reports about British increases in displacement and gun calibre were not yet confirmed and he was reluctant to be the one driving the escalation of the arms race.

During the winter of 1906–07, there was little further progress as the RMA waited for the Reichstag elections in January 1907. Then, early in 1907, it was learned that the US Navy was planning a 20,000-tonne battleship with 10 x 12in guns, the later *Delaware*. The five turrets were to be on the centre-line, just as with *Michigan*. Now Tirpitz abandoned his caution of the previous months. At a conference in March 1907, he gave the order to the Construction Department to prepare a design study for an improved *Nassau* class with 30.5cm guns and belt armour of 320mm. The cost for this design was estimated at around 46 million gold marks. The calibre question was finally settled when the chief of the General Navy Department pointed out that the 30.5cm calibre must be adopted before or at the same time as the new Fleet Law amendment, otherwise the question could be deferred for years.

With the calibre question resolved, only the arrangement of the turrets remained to be finalized. A report from London about two Brazilian battleships being constructed in Britain threw new light on this question. The so-called 'Brazilian arrangement' (two turrets forward, two turrets aft, and one turret on each beam) allowed for a heavier broadside although the same number of cannon were shipped, and suddenly the German hexagon arrangement seemed antiquated. Tirpitz was convinced, but his Department chiefs were not so easily swayed and clung to the

An aerial view of *Helgoland* shows the same hexagonal arrangement of the turrets as with the previous class.

idea of a 'lee reserve' and 'advantages for battle to both sides'. Likewise, it was considered that the American arrangement of superfiring turret groups (one turret mounted above and behind the other) could lead to a single hit disabling two turrets. Tirpitz considered the arguments and finally decided to retain the hexagon arrangement.

On propulsion, the question was not whether to install turbines, but rather when. Once again it came down to a question of cost. Turbines were more expensive for the time being because, among other things, of a one million gold mark royalty payment per unit to Parsons. Beginning in 1910, other companies would have developed turbines and Parsons would no longer have a monopoly. Tirpitz therefore decided to defer the question of turbines until the following year.

On 13 February 1908, Kaiser Wilhelm II signed the construction order for the battleships of 1908, the *Helgoland* class. The first three ships were to be included in the budget of 1908, while *Oldenburg* would belong to the budget of 1909. As with the previous class, the building contracts were put out to tender. The *Ostfriesland* was awarded to the Imperial Dockyard, Wilhelmshaven, without tender, while *Helgoland* and *Thüringen* were offered to private yards by tender. The successful bidders were Howaldtswerke in Kiel and A.G. Weser in Bremen. Howaldt had offered an especially low tender to ensure gaining the contract, and their successful negotiation saved the company from bankruptcy. As a consolation, Tirpitz awarded the battleship for the 1909 budget, *Oldenburg*, to Ferdinand Schichau, Danzig, before the budget had even been approved by the Reichstag. Even though no payment had been made, Schichau began to order materials and make preparations for laying the keel. This activity had the effect of giving the appearance that Germany was building ships at an even more accelerated rate and led to panic in London. This panic led to the 'we want eight and we won't wait' campaign in the British press, and by April 1910 eight capital ships had been laid down in British shipyards. The German secrecy had inadvertently led to an escalation in the naval arms race.

Ostfriesland	Weight (tonnes)	Weight as percentage of displacement (tonnes)
Ship hull	6,779	30.7
Armour	8,082	36.8
Engines	1,745	7.9
Armament	3,334	15.1
Outfitting	971	4.4
Fuel	1,170	5.3
Construction displacement	22,081	

	Helgoland	Ostfriesland	Thüringen	Oldenburg
Building dockyard	Howaldts, Kiel	Imperial, Wilhelmshaven	A.G. Weser, Bremen.	Ferdinand Schichau, Danzig.
Building number	500	31	166	828
Keel laying	19 October 1908	19 October 1908	2 November 1908	1 March 1909
Launched	25 September 1909	30 September 1909	27 November 1909	30 June 1910
Commissioned	23 August 1911	1 August 1911	1 July 1911	1 May 1912
Displacement (tonnes)	Designed: 22,808 Loaded: 24,700	Designed: 22,808 Loaded: 24,700	Designed: 22,808 Loaded: 24,700	Designed: 22,808 Loaded: 24,700
Length (metres)	167.2	167.2	167.2	167.2
Beam (metres)	28.5	28.5	28.5	28.5
Draught (metres)	Construction: 8.68 Loaded: 8.94	Construction: 8.68 Loaded: 8.94	Construction: 8.68 Loaded: 8.94	Construction: 8.68 Loaded: 8.94
Moulded depth (metres)	13.38	13.38	13.38	13.38
Performance (indicated horsepower)	Designed: 28,000 Maximum: 31,258	Designed: 28,000 Maximum: 35,500	Designed: 28,000 Maximum: 34,944	Designed: 28,000 Maximum: 34,394
Revolutions per minute	125	126	117	120
Speed (knots)	Designed: 20.5 Maximum: 20.8	Designed: 20.5 Maximum: 21.2	Designed: 20.5 Maximum: 21.0	Designed: 20.5 Maximum: 21.3
Fuel (tonnes) – fuel oil from 1915	Construction: 900 Maximum: 3,200 Fuel oil: 197	Construction: 900 Maximum: 3,200 Fuel oil: 197	Construction: 900 Maximum: 3,200 Fuel oil: 197	Construction: 900 Maximum: 3,200 Fuel oil: 197
Range: nautical miles	5,500 at 10 knots	5,500 at 10 knots	5,500 at 10 knots	5,500 at 10 knots
Cost (million Gold Marks)	46.196	43.597	46.314	45.801
Compartments	17	17	17	17
Double bottom (as percentage of length)	86	86	86	86
Crew	42 officers 1,071 men	42 officers 1,071 men; as flagship a further 13 officers and 66 men	42 officers 1,071 men	42 officers 1,071 men

SMS *WESTFALEN* AND SMS *RHEINLAND* OFF ECKERÖ

In early 1918, the Finnish Svinhufuud provisional government requested German assistance to free Finland from the grip of Russia and the Bolsheviks. The German response was to dispatch a 'Special Unit' of battleships and other vessels to occupy the Aland Islands, to use as an advanced base for the intervention in Hangö and then Helsingfors. On 5 March, *Westfalen* and *Rheinland* arrived off Eckerö and to their surprise found the Swedish ships *Sverige*, *Thor* and *Oscar II* were already anchored on the roadstead and Swedish troops were ashore. Staff officers were dispatched on foot across the ice to negotiate with the Swedish troops and prevent needless bloodshed, but meanwhile a Finnish pilot arrived and guided the German warships close inshore, where they anchored between the Swedish ships and the shoreline. A treaty was arranged and the Germans were able to continue with their further occupation and liberation of Finland.

Our battle scene shows *Westfalen* and *Rheinland* in the ice between *Sverige*, *Oscar II* and the shore at Eckerö. By the evening of 7 March, all the troops were ashore and the first phase of the operation was complete. The advance continued and on 3 April Hangö was taken by troops landed and supported by *Westfalen* and *Posen*. The Red forces were quickly defeated. The third phase followed quickly so that on 11 April the German forces arrived off Helsingfors and after several days of street fighting the city was liberated from the Bolshevik forces. The action in Finland showed that the battleships of the High Sea Fleet were an important weapon able to execute freely the political will of the German government.

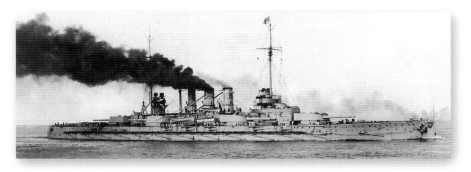

After being placed in service, the battleship *Ostfriesland* served continuously as flagship of the commander of Squadron I from April 1912. This pre-war photograph shows *Ostfriesland* in this role. The funnels were later increased in height.

Armament

The main armament of the *Helgoland* class was the new 30.5cm SK L/50 Drh.L C/08, once again mounted in a hexagonal arrangement. At the request of the director of the Weapons Department, 50-calibre long barrels were chosen instead of the 45-calibre L/45. These cannon brought a significant increase in performance for only a small increase in weight. All the turrets featured built-in rangefinders and had a working chamber that rotated with the turret. The guns were hydraulically elevated, and the turrets were trained electrically. The maximum elevation of 13.5° allowed the 405kg armour-piercing shell to be fired out to 180hm. After modification to produce an elevation of 16°, the range was improved to 20.4hm. The centre-line turrets carried an outfit of 90 shells per gun, but the wing turrets were restricted to 75 shells per barrel because of space limitations in the shell rooms. As with all German munitions during World War I, the propellant charge came in two parts, a fore charge and a main charge. The fore charge was in a silk bag and consisted of 34.5kg of RP C/12 cordite. ('RP' denoted 'tubular powder propellant'.) The main charge came in a brass cartridge case with an igniter and consisted of 91kg of RP C/12. These charges allowed the armour-piercing shell to be fired at a muzzle velocity of 855mps, and the rate of fire was a rapid three rounds per minute. For each turret there was a projectile chamber on the upper platform deck. For the three aft turrets, the two powder chambers (magazines) were on the lower platform deck, as were the seven powder chambers associated with the three forward turrets. The average barrel life was around 200 rounds, far in excess of rival navies' guns.

The medium-calibre artillery consisted of 14 x 15cm SK L/45 C/06 cannon in pivot mounts protected in armoured casemates. These cannon were ranged to 135hm, but after 1915 the range was increased out to 168hm. The total ammunition outfit was 2,100 shells. The weight of the projectile was 45.3kg and could fire at a rate of fire of 3–4 rounds per minute. Even with the high muzzle velocity of 835mps, the barrel life was still approximately 1,400 rounds.

A total of 14 x 8.8cm SK L/45 torpedo-boat defence cannon were mounted in the hull and superstructure. From these a 9kg shell could be fired at a muzzle velocity of 890mps, and an outfit of 2,400 shells was carried. Nevertheless, in 1914 two of these guns on the aft superstructure were replaced with two 8.8cm Flak L/45 C/13 cannon.

A close-up of *Ostfriesland*'s bridge shows the heavy, medium and light artillery. The bridgework is simple and formed mainly by canvas dodgers, including the admiral's bridge.

The Imperial Navy placed great faith in the torpedo as an offensive weapon, and the *Helgoland* class carried a total of six underwater 50cm torpedo tubes, four on the beam and a bow and stern tube. The torpedo carried was the 50cm diameter G/6c torpedo. This had a length of 6m and carried a warhead weighing 160kg. The range of this weapon was 5,000m at 27 knots and 2,200m at 35 knots. A total of 16 torpedoes were carried. The battleships also had eight 110cm searchlights.

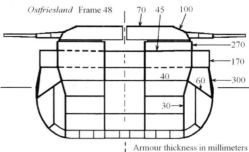

Ostfriesland Frame 48

Armour thickness in millimeters

Armour

The *Helgoland* class carried thicker armour than the preceding class. The main belt was finally decided at 300mm, tapering to 170mm at its upper and lower extremities. The casemate armour was also 170mm. The bow armour was 120mm, with no tapering, and the aft armour was 120mm, tapering to 100mm above and below. The main belt and citadel were enclosed by two armoured transverse bulkheads each of 210mm thickness. The armoured deck above the casemates was 45mm thick whilst the main armoured deck was 40mm thick for the horizontal deck, and the sloping deck (Böschung) was 60mm thick. An armoured torpedo bulkhead ran the length of the citadel and was 30mm thick. The armoured barbettes varied in thickness with the maximum thickness being 300mm. The turret faces were also 300mm thick, the sides 270mm. The horizontal roofs were 70mm thick, and the sloping turret armour was 100mm thick. The conning tower was extremely heavily armoured with a maximum thickness of 400mm, and the armoured shaft to the central control position was 100mm thick. The aft conning tower was less heavily armoured with a maximum thickness of 200mm. As was usual the armour was Krupp cemented steel.

As originally envisaged the belt armour of the *Helgoland* class was to be 320mm thick, but by the time the final draft was completed this had been reduced to 300mm. This, however, was still 20mm thicker than contemporary British and American ships. The wing passage, protective bunker and torpedo bulkhead are clearly shown.

Seakeeping

Helgoland had a metacentric height of 2.6m. They were known as good sea ships and *Ostfriesland* had little trouble crossing the Atlantic in 1920, when she was allocated to the United States. However, the high metacentric height meant that the rolling movements were harsh. The ships manoeuvred well and had a small turning circle – speed loss with hard rudder was 65 per cent, and a heel over of 7° could be expected. In a heavy swell the loss of speed was slight.

Machinery

Steam was provided by 15 naval coal-fired boilers working at a pressure of 16 atmospheres, or 235psi. The boilers were fitted with supplemental oil firing from 1915. The boilers were arranged in three divided boiler rooms, the

Ostfriesland getting up steam in the aft two boiler rooms.

Ostfriesland undergoing routine maintenance in a floating dock in Kiel late in the war

foremost boiler room having three boilers, the remaining two having six boilers each. In the Imperial Navy, the boiler rooms were numbered from aft, as were the frame numbers, therefore the aftmost boiler room was I Boiler Room.

To provide the extra power for the increased displacement, the ships of this class had three four-cylinder, triple-expansion engines, arranged in three adjacent engine rooms. Each engine drove a 5.1m-diameter propeller. As with all German ships of the period, the designed horsepower was exceeded during trials. The two rudders were mounted parallel to each another. There were two steam-driven rudder engines, interconnected and driving two screw drive mechanisms. There was also provision to work the rudders by hand.

The freshwater plant had four Pape & Henneberg evaporators with a minimum output of 200 tonnes per day, but the achieved performance was 194 tonnes of boiler feed water and 102 tonnes of fresh water. Electrical power was provided by eight turbo-dynamos with an output of 2,000kW at 225 volts. The four generators of the aft station were located on the upper platform deck to port and starboard between frames 28 and 34, and the forward four were located on the lower platform deck, between frames 90 and 100, to port and starboard.

General characteristics and changes

Artillery observation positions were added to the masts after the beginning of the war. The 8.8cm guns were removed and their apertures were welded up. Compass pedestals aft of the main mast were removed in 1915. During the war, the galley chimneys were extended upwards and forwards, and ran a short distance up the main mast.

All the ships of this class had their funnels extended in length. In 1913, *Oldenburg* had her funnel extended 3m, from 18.5m to 21.5m. Likewise, in 1913 *Thüringen* had her funnels extended 1.5m to 20m high. In 1915 *Helgoland* followed with a 1.5m increase to 20m, and finally in 1917 *Ostfriesland* also had a 1.5m increase to 20m high.

Service record

Helgoland

Namesake: German island in the German Bight. In 1890 Germany exchanged extensive areas in German East Africa to Britain for the island.

The keel was laid down in Howaldts Dockyard, Kiel, in the autumn of 1908 and *Helgoland* was launched from the cradle on 25 September 1909. Trials began

SMS *HELGOLAND*

The *Helgoland* class was the second generation of German dreadnought battleships. They represented the biggest single step in development in both size and cost. The ships retained the wasteful hexagonal arrangement for the turrets, even though State Secretary Tirpitz was now convinced there was a better solution to this problem. Gun calibre, however, was increased to 30.5cm, as this calibre was now available in a quick-firing model. The employment of a 50-calibre-length gun gave this weapon an excellent muzzle velocity and striking power. The *Helgoland* class served throughout the war in I Squadron and gave sterling service. The ineffectiveness of the mine hit on *Ostfriesland* on 1 June 1916 once again showed the quality of the underwater protective system against contemporary weapons.

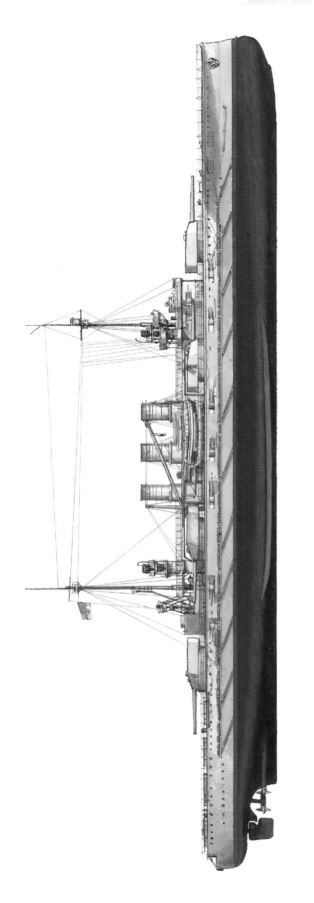
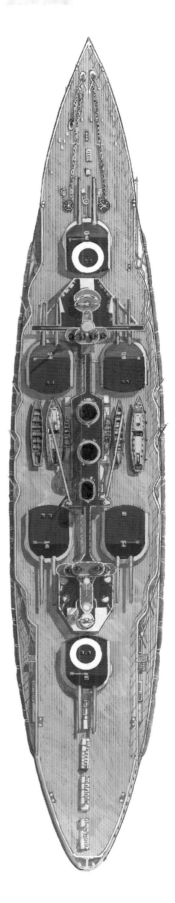

in August 1911 and the ship was commissioned on 23 August. By 9 December 1909, the trials were concluded and on 20 December she replaced *Hannover* in I Squadron. Fleet manoeuvres followed in the North Sea in March

A view of *Helgoland* in the North Sea later in the war. The anti-torpedo nets have been removed and the funnels increased in height.

1912, then in November 1912 the fleet conducted more exercises in the North Sea plus in the Skagerrak and Kattegat. The exercises the following year were basically the same, but a visit to Norway was included.

After war began, *Helgoland* participated in the fleet advances and operations of 2–3 November 1914 and 15–16 December 1914, and in 1915 those on 29–30 March, 17–18 April, 21–22 April, 17–18 May and 29–30 May, without any notable incidents taking place. In August 1915 she was part of the covering force for the Riga Gulf operation. Further fleet operations followed on 11–12 September, 23–24 October and 16 December 1915. On 4 March 1916, she took part in the operation to welcome *Möwe* home to the Amrumbank passage. Further operations followed on 5–7 March, 25–26 March, 21–22 April and 24–25 April 1916.

During the Skagerrak battle on 31 May 1916, *Helgoland* received a 13.5in shell hit in the forecastle at 2015hrs. The shell struck above the bow torpedo tube, where the armour was 150mm thick, and was holed, 80 tonnes of water eventually entering the ship. There were no losses in men. During the night battle on 1 June, *Helgoland* took part in defending against the British destroyers and sank one of the attackers. After returning to Wilhelmshaven, repairs were carried out in the dockyard there from 3 to 16 June. *Helgoland* took part in the advances on 18–20 August 1916 and 18–20 October 1916.

When leaving the dock at Wilhelmshaven in April 1917, *Helgoland* rammed the almost complete battlecruiser *Hindenburg*, which was in the fitting-out basin, and was slightly damaged. In October she and *Oldenburg* went to Amrumbank to meet the two cruisers *Bremse* and *Brummer*, and on 27 October 1917 she went to the Baltic, but did not participate in the conquest of the Baltic Islands. From Putziger Wiek, she was detached to Kiel and from 8 November was again conducting security and picket duties in the North Sea. During 1918 there were increased operations for the security of minesweeper flotillas. *Helgoland* also took part in the advance of 23–25 April 1918.

Helgoland was not among the ships interned under the conditions of the Armistice. From 21 to 22 November 1918, she undertook a trip to Harwich to collect the crews of interned U-boats. Subsequently, she was put out of service on 16 December 1918 and was stricken from the list of warships on 5 November 1919. On 5 August 1920 she was delivered to Great Britain and was wrecked by 1924.

A view of *Ostfriesland* in a Norwegian fjord before the war in 1913. Norway offered to host the interned German ships after the Armistice, but the Allies would have none of it.

Ostfriesland

Namesake: Area between the mouth of the River Ems and Oldenburg.

The keel for *Ostfriesland* was struck on 19 October 1908. Provision was made for a Squadron Staff. She was launched on 30 September 1909 and placed in service on 1 August

1911. The trials were quickly concluded by 15 September, so that on 22 September *Ostfriesland* could be incorporated into I Squadron. Individual ship training followed and then squadron and fleet exercises in November. On 24 April 1912, *Ostfriesland* replaced *Westfalen* as squadron flagship.

Ostfriesland took part in all the fleet manoeuvres and cruises up to the beginning of the war. With the outbreak of war, the squadron prematurely broke off the cruise to Norway and arrived in Wilhelmshaven on 29 July 1914. In October, *Ostfriesland* received two 8.8cm Flak guns. The squadron took part in the operations of 2–3 November 1914 and 15–16 December 1914. In the battle of the Dogger Bank, I Squadron was ordered to raise steam at 1200hrs and at 1233hrs I and II Squadrons raised anchor and put to sea to support the cruisers. They were too late, and at 1905hrs dropped anchor on Schillig Roads, without having made contact with the enemy.

From 22 February to 13 March 1915, I Squadron returned to the Baltic for training. After that the squadron took part in advances on 29–30 March (without *Westfalen* and *Nassau*), 17–18 April, 21–22 April, 17–18 May (without *Rheinland* and *Posen*) and finally on 29–30 May 1915. On 4 August, I Squadron again sailed to the Baltic to undergo training, and a few days later served as covering group for the attack on the Riga Gulf. On 26 August, the squadron returned to Wilhelmshaven and on 11–12 September they took part in a fleet advance, without *Posen*, *Nassau* and *Oldenburg*. A further advance was undertaken on 23–24 October 1915, this time without *Helgoland*.

On 5–7 March 1916, I Squadron made an advance, without *Rheinland*, followed by advances on 21–22 March, 25 and 26 March, and 24–25 April. During the Skagerrak battle, *Ostfriesland* fired on British light cruisers and the battleship *Warspite*. She also set an enemy destroyer on fire. During the return journey, at 0620hrs she struck a mine, which caused the flooding of some coal bunkers, so that eventually there were 400 tonnes of water in the ship. Losses amounted to one dead and ten wounded. From 2 June to 25 July, *Ostfriesland* lay in the Imperial Dockyard, Wilhelmshaven, for repairs.

From 18 to 20 August 1916, I Squadron undertook an advance, and on 25–26 September 1916 covered an advance by the II Führer der Torpedoboote (Leader of Torpedo Boats) to Terschelling Bank. A further Fleet advance followed to the Dogger Bank on 18–20 October.

The year 1917 saw increased activity for the German battleships on picket duty and covering minesweeping forces, as the British heavy forces abandoned the North Sea and decided on a mine offensive instead. During the conquest of the Baltic Islands, the 2nd Division of I Squadron went to the Baltic to guard against any incursion by British forces. On 28 October, *Ostfriesland*, *Helgoland*, *Thüringen* and *Oldenburg* arrived in Putzig Wiek and from there *Ostfriesland* and *Thüringen* went to Arensburg, where they arrived on 29 October. They were no longer required, however, and the Special Unit was dissolved on 2 November 1917, so the ships began the rear march.

For the last fleet advance on 23–24 April 1918, I Squadron consisted of only *Ostfriesland*, *Thüringen*, *Helgoland*, *Oldenburg* and *Nassau*, as the other ships were absent in the Baltic. On 8 August, *Ostfriesland*, *Thüringen* and *Nassau* themselves formed a Special Unit for Operation *Schlußstein*, the

An aerial view of *Ostfriesland* taken during the war with turrets trained to port 90°. This photograph must have been taken in October 1917 when the 2nd Admiral of Squadron I, Konteradmiral Freiherr von Dalwigk zu Lichtenfels was aboard, as indicated by the Konteradmiral's flag at the foremast.

ABOVE
Changing a gun barrel on *Ostfriesland* during the war. The cone-shaped devices are indicators for the position of the rudders, the left being red and the right green.

ABOVE RIGHT
Thüringen at a practice shoot during the war before the Skagerrak battle.

planned operation to occupy St Petersburg. The unit arrived in the western Baltic on 10 August, but, as we have seen, the operation was overtaken by events and was cancelled. On 21 August, the three battleships were dismissed and on 23 August arrived back in Wilhelmshaven.

Ostfriesland stood ready for the cancelled fleet advance of 30 October 1918, and after that went to the Elbe mouth on 3 November. On 6 November, the mutinous crew took over command. *Ostfriesland* was decommissioned on 16 December 1918 and then served as an accommodation ship.

Following the Armistice, *Ostfriesland* was not interned, but on 7 April 1920 went to Rosyth with a German crew where on 9 April she was taken over by an American crew and was transferred to the United States. She was sunk off Cape Henry, Virginia, in bombing trials on 21 July 1921.

Thüringen

Namesake: Province in central Germany.

Thüringen's keel was laid at A.G. Weser in Bremen on 2 November 1908. Launching followed on 27 November 1909 and after completion *Thüringen* was towed down the River Weser with the aid of six pontoon barges to reduce her draught. On 1 July 1911 she was commissioned and acceptance trials were completed on 10 September. On 19 September, she joined I Squadron in Wilhelmshaven and participated in all the exercises and manoeuvres of the fleet.

From the beginning of the war until July 1915, *Thüringen* was present in all operations by I Squadron, and also participated in the Riga Gulf operation in August 1915 as part of the covering force, before returning to the North Sea. *Thüringen* participated in the Skagerrak battle in 1916. During the night battle she was mainly responsible for the destruction of the British armoured cruiser *Black Prince*. The battleship suffered no personnel losses.

 SMS *THÜRINGEN* IN NIGHT BATTLE

Soon after 0100hrs on the morning of 1 June 1916, the battleships *Nassau* and *Thüringen* sighted a vessel with four funnels to port ahead. The stranger did not answer the recognition signal, but turned away to starboard. A searchlight was illuminated and a British armoured cruiser, the *Black Prince*, was recognized at a range of 1,000m. *Thüringen* opened fire immediately and of the ten heavy, 27 medium and 24 light artillery projectiles fired, scarcely a shot missed and *Black Prince* was raked from stem to stern. Flames swept across the ship to the height of the mast. Then *Ostfriesland* and *Nassau* joined the firing, followed finally by *Friedrich der Große*. The German battleships swept past and left the cruiser a glowing wreck, marked by several detonations, before a single powerful explosion sent *Black Prince* to the depths. Just as the destruction of *Pommern* demonstrated that older-generation ships were inadequately protected against underwater weapons, the destruction of *Black Prince* and other British armoured cruisers showed that the type was totally insufficient against even medium-calibre cannon at shorter ranges.

Thüringen took part in the fleet advance of 18–20 August 1916, but missed the advance of 18–20 October 1916 because of damage to her rudder. During the conquest of the Baltic Islands, *Thüringen* went to the Baltic on 28 October 1917 and on 29 October arrived on Arensburg Roads. It was no longer required, however, and began the return journey on 2 November 1917.

In 1918 *Thüringen* took part in the last fleet advance of the war, on 23–25 April 1918. From 12 to 22 August she was assigned to the Special Unit for Operation *Schlußstein*, under the command of Vizeadmiral Boedicker. When this operation was cancelled, *Thüringen* returned to the North Sea.

Thüringen was one of the ships that assembled on Schillig Roads for the fleet advance planned for 30 October 1918. It is to her lasting discredit that revolutionary unrest broke out aboard her as one of the first ships, and the mutinous stokers extinguished the fires in her boilers. The torpedo boats B110 and B112 went alongside, while the U-boat *U135* trained her guns on the mutinous ship. A total of 314 seamen and 124 stokers were arrested and thus the mutiny was at first stopped, but the revolution could not be prevented.

On 16 December 1918, *Thüringen* was decommissioned. She was not interned and remained an accommodation ship. Later she was handed to France and transferred to Cherbourg on 29 April 1920. The French Navy used her as a target and large parts of the hull still exist off the French coast in relatively intact condition.

Oldenburg

Namesake: German Duchy, today part of Lower Saxony.

Just as with Goeben in 1908, the RMA signed a preliminary agreement for the building of this ship, this time with Ferdinand Schichau of Danzig. Tirpitz did this for commercial considerations, among other things, to fix building costs and thus avoid possible later price increases. When the British learned of this manoeuvre, they speculated that Germany was building ships in excess of the official set number, and the resulting jingoism was enough to spawn a massive naval building programme.

The Schichau Dockyard struck the keel on 1 March 1909 and on 30 June 1910 the launching took place. *Oldenburg* was transferred to Kiel for final fitting out and was commissioned on 1 May 1912, joining I Squadron on 17 July 1912. In July and August she took part in the exercises and manoeuvres of the fleet.

After the outbreak of war, *Oldenburg* took part in all the operations of I Squadron, including the Riga operation in August 1915, but did not participate in the fleet advance of 11–12 September 1915.

In the Skagerrak battle, *Oldenburg* fought in the day battle against the British line, and then took an active part in the night battle. During an engagement with the 4th Flotilla, she sank a destroyer, but received a shell hit on a searchlight position above the bridge. As the ship was being directed from outside the armoured conning tower, a total of seven men were killed and 14 were wounded, including the ship's commander. The 1st Officer, Korvettenkapitän Vollmer, took over guidance of the ship and averted a collision with the next ship ahead. After returning from the battle, *Oldenburg* remained on picket and security duties and only went for repairs in Wilhelmshaven from 30 June to 15 July 1916. *Oldenburg* took part in the fleet advance of 18–20 August 1916 and subsequent operations.

An aerial view of *Oldenburg* late in the war in the North Sea. The greater beam of German battleships is well displayed here.

On 18 October 1917, *Oldenburg* covered the return of the cruisers *Brummer* and *Bremse* after their successful mission against convoy traffic between Scotland and Norway. Later, on 27 October, she went to the Putzig Wiek in the Baltic to relieve III and IV Squadrons after the conquest of the Baltic Islands, but this was not required and she returned to the North Sea.

Oldenburg took part in the last fleet advance on 22–25 April 1918. When the battlecruiser *Moltke* fell out with engine damage, *Oldenburg* was detached to the damaged ship and took her in tow. During the evening, the hawser broke but was repaired after one hour. After being towed right across the North Sea, the tow was slipped on the afternoon of 25 April at approximately the latitude of List. The performance of *Oldenburg* during the operation was given particular credit by the fleet chief.

From 11 August to 5 October 1918, *Oldenburg* underwent annual refit in Wilhelmshaven and at the end of October stood ready for the abortive fleet operation. *Oldenburg* was not interned after the Armistice, but was later ceded to Japan. In June 1920 she was sold to a British scrap company and was wrecked in Dordrecht in 1921.

BIBLIOGRAPHY

Breyer, Siegfried, *Marine Arsenal Band 17, Nassau und Helgoland* (Friedburg, 1991)

Breyer, Siegfried, *Marine Arsenal Band 45, Deutschland Klasse* (Friedburg, 1999)

Campbell, John, *Jutland* (Conway, 1986)

Evers, Heinrich, *Kriegsschiffbau* (Berlin, 1943)

Greißmer, Alex, *Linienschiffe der Kaiserlichen Marine 1906–1918* (Bernard & Graefe, 1999)

Gröner, Erich, *Die deutschen Kriegsschiffe 1815–1945* (Bernard & Graefe, 1982)

Hildebrand, Hans, *Die Deutschen Kriegsschiffe*, Vols 1–7 (Koehlers, 1979)

Koop, Gerhard and Klaus-Peter Schmolke, *Von der Nassau zur König Klasse* (Bernard & Graefe, 1999)

Mantey, Eberhard von, *Auf See unbesiegt*, Vols 1 and 2 (J. F. Lehmans, 1922)

Mantey, Eberhard von, *Der Krieg zur See 1914–1918: Der Krieg in der Nordsee*, Vols 1–7 (E.S. Mittler & Sohn, 1920–64)

Mantey, Eberhard von, *Der Krieg zur See 1914–1918: Der Krieg in der Ostsee*, Vols 1–3 (E.S. Mittler & Sohn, 1920–64)

Mukhenikov, V.B., *German Battleships Part 1* (St Petersburg, 2005)

Philbin, Tobias, *Warship Profile 37*, SMS König (Profile, 1973)

Strohbusch, E., *Marine Rundschau 1978/7 Nassau* (J.F. Lehmans, 1978)

Strohbusch, E., *Marine Rundschau 1979/6 Bayern* (J.F. Lehmans, 1979)

INDEX